DESIGNING GRAPHIC ILLUSIONS

SendPoints

DESIGNING GRAPHIC ILLUSIONS

SendPoints

EDITED & PUBLISHED BY SendPoints Publishing Co., Ltd.
PUBLISHER: Lin Gengli
PUBLISHING DIRECTOR: Lin Shijian
ASSISTANT PUBLISHING-DIRECTOR: Chen Ting
CHIEF EDITOR: Lin Shijian
LEAD EDITOR: Huang Shaojun
EXECUTIVE EDITOR: Zeng Wanting
DESIGN DIRECTOR: Lin Shijian
EXECUTIVE ART EDITOR: Lai Yujie
PROOFREADING: James N. Powell

REGISTERED ADDRESS: Room 15A Block 9 Tsui Chuk Garden, Wong Tai Sin, Kowloon, Hong Kong
TEL: +852-35832323 / FAX: +852-35832448
OFFICE ADDRESS: 7F, 9th Anning Street, Jinshazhou, Baiyun District, Guangzhou, China
TEL: +86-20-89095121 / FAX: +86-20-89095206
BEIJING OFFICE: Room 107, Floor 1, Xiyingfang Alley, Ande Road, Dongcheng District, Beijing, China
TEL: +86-10-84139071 / FAX: +86-10-84139071
SHANGHAI OFFICE: Room 307, Building 1, Hong Qiang Creative, Zhabei District, Shanghai, China
TEL: +86-21-63523469 / FAX: +86-21-63523469

SALES MANAGER: Kris Guo
TEL: +86-20-81007895
EMAIL: sales@sendpoints.cn
WEBSITE: www.sendpoints.cn / www.spbooks.cn

ISBN 978-988-79283-5-5

Printed and bound in China.

FOREWORD

After centuries of development, visual illusion has evolved from a natural phenomenon into a specialized field of art. Whereas Medieval artists made use of visual illusions to create famous paintings and design grand palaces, contemporary designers have used illusions to deceive the eyes and distort perceptions. Compared with other art forms, visual illusion art uniquely attracts public attention. Moreover, because of visual illusion, many designers have become devoted to the design industry.

Since childhood I have been passionate about optical illusion. When visiting the Cathedral of Naples for the first time, I was shocked by the perspective fresco *Gloria del Paradiso*, created by the Italian painter Giovanni Lanfranco (1582-1647). The way the fresco magically deceived my visual, perceptions, and emotions made me realize that there are many compelling forms of this art. Since then, I have begun to seriously explore and study masters of optical illusion: Andrea Pozzo (1642-1709) in Rome, Correggio (1489-1534) in Parma, Giulio Romano (1499-1546) in Mantua, and Donato Bramante's (1444-1514) anamorphosis in bas-relief of the Church of San Satiro, in Milan.

Throughout the long history of art, there have been many artists who were able to combine painting, sculpture, and graphics with the charming elegance of mathematics. Dozens of perspective theories have given us the opportunity to study and explore the fascinating world of optical illusion. And numerous artists have applied these theories in their works, such as Italian architect Giacomo Barozzi da Vignola (1507-1573), German painter Albrecht Dürer (1471-1528), Italian painter and architect Cigoli (1559-1613), Italian Renaissance sculptor Vincenzo Danti (1530-1576), and famous Dutch graphic artist M. C. Escher (1898-1972). As modern artists, instead of creating artworks using only the traditional classic approach, we have evolved to using lenses, cameras, and modern technology, all of which can help us to speed up the complex process of creating various optical illusions.

My passion for street art has evolved over 25 years. In the beginning, it was only about painting on the road, using only simple chalk, and taking only a few hours. However, with the development of anamorphic perspective and the increasing interaction and involvement of the public, street art has become more like a science fiction film: overflowing with special effects. Whether a sketch on paper or artwork on a wall or street, optical illusion can be presented anywhere, in any form, without any limits. When making art we should pay attention to integrating painting with the ambient environment. Lights, textures, shadows, and colors present in the scene provide the elements that guide every single choice in the process of creation. And each choice is related to the colors, shapes, and lights of the subject. Simply neglecting even one of these elements, the illusion may lose its charm and vitality. Recently, thanks to technology and experiences gathered from the past, visual illusion has enjoyed an exponential growth in popularity, permeating almost all artistic fields. Numerous designers have tried to stimulate their imaginations and challenge their vision through illusions: making the impossible possible.

I am deeply grateful to the publisher for including me among the fine artists in this volume. Over the years, I have been the guest of several magazines and books whose themes are similar to those found herein. This volume, however, is the most complete and most systematic work about graphic illusion, and it offers an excellent tool both for study and for research, both for insiders and for curious enthusiasts.

Cuboliquido

Cuboliquido is an Italian 3-D street painter who was the first artist to combine experiments with anamorphic 3-D art and animated video with video-mapping. He was the first prize winner of the Dubai Canvas Awards (2017). Cuboliquido has also been commissioned by world-famous companies—including Disney, Universal Cinema, Warner Bros., Amazon, Coca-Cola, Samsung, Unilever, Expo Milano 2015, Tiffany & Co., and many more—to create 3-D street paintings.

CONTENTS

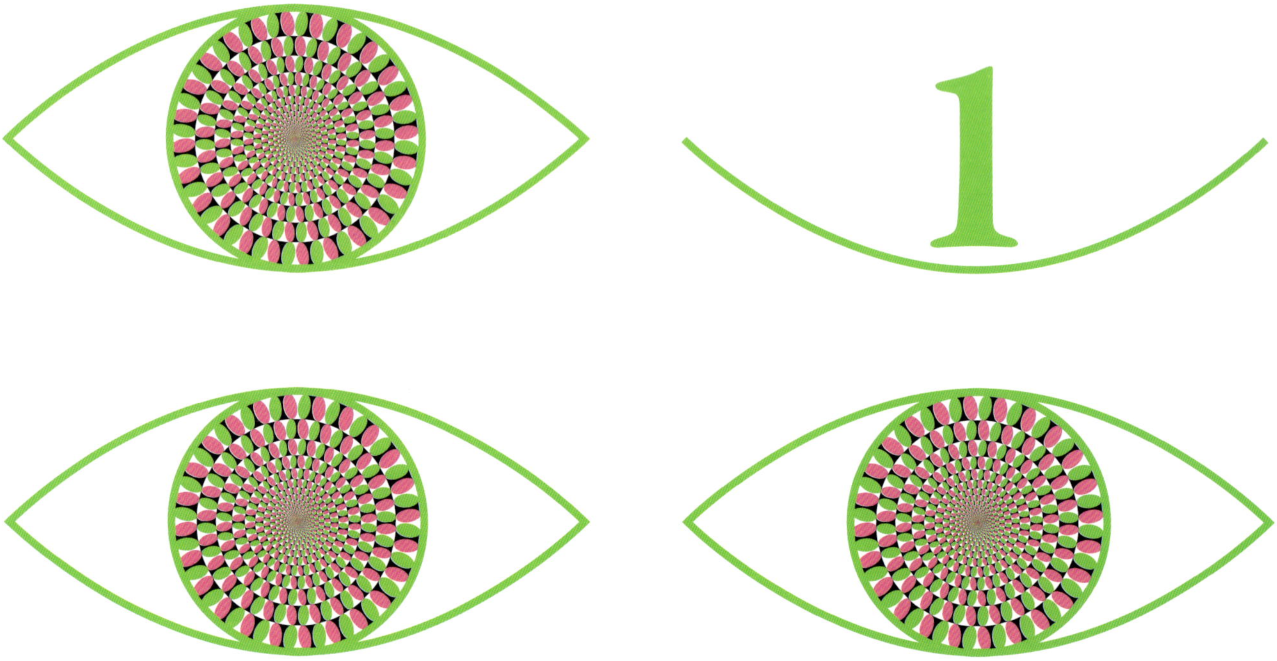

1

VISUAL ILLUSION

From mirage, to motion blur, perspective architecture, and surreal paintings, visual illusion has been around us for thousands of years. However, it took humans a eons to recognize it and learn to use it in artistic creations. This wonderful history can be traced back to ancient times.

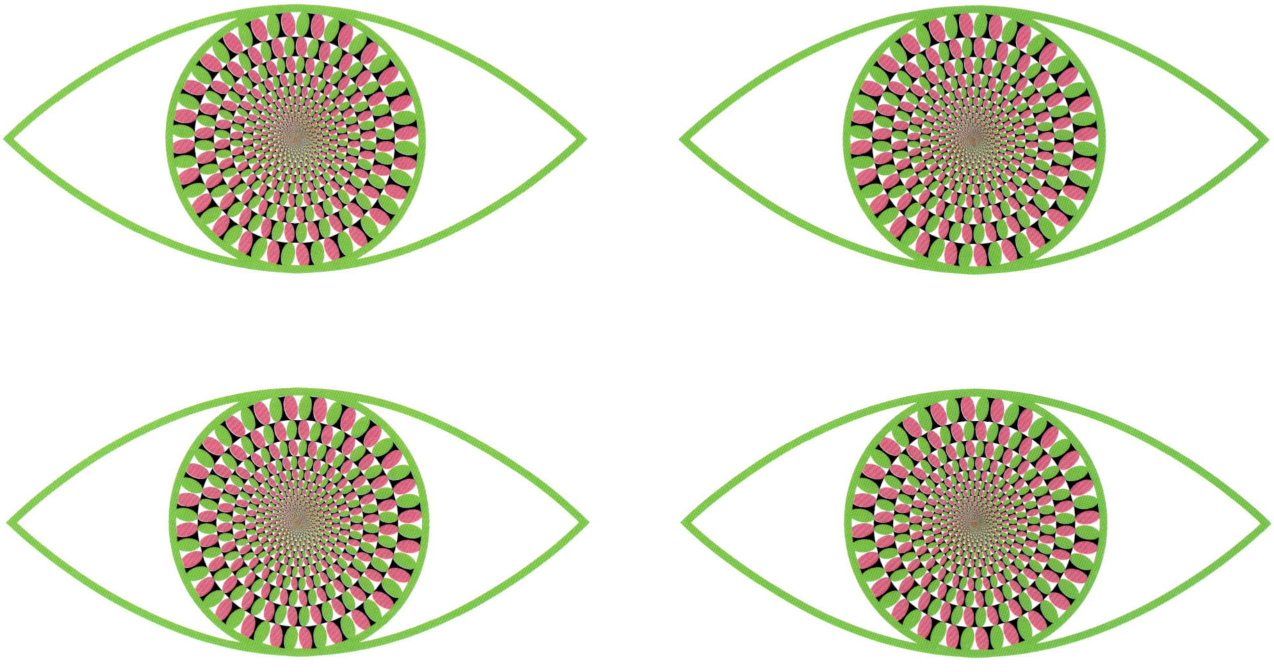

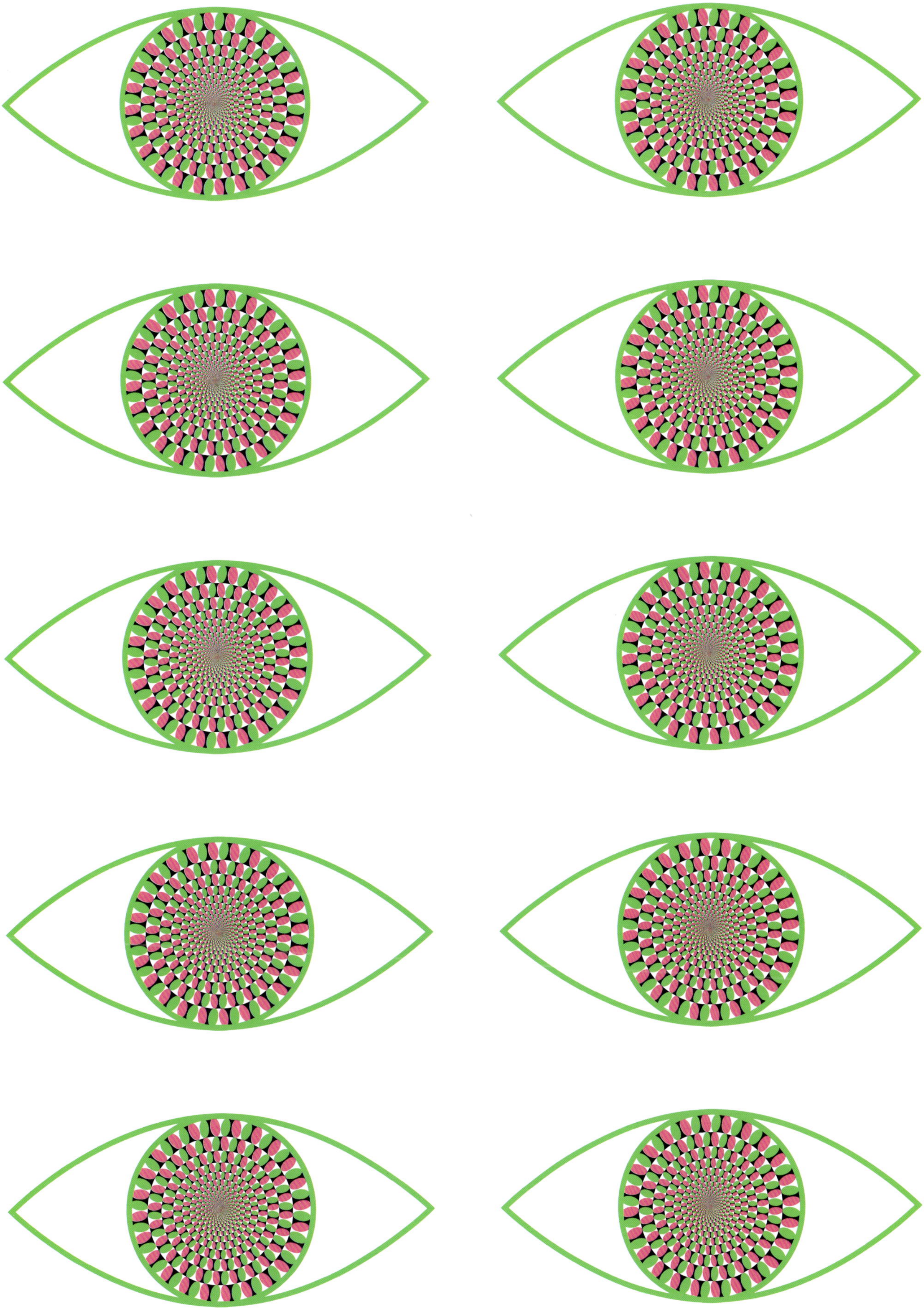

WHAT IS VISUAL ILLUSION

Seeing is not believing. As early as ancient times, mankind knew that direct perception does not always reflect the real world. Mankind found that seen objects sometimes appear differently than they do in reality. We call such differences visual illusions.
Visual illusions (also called optical illusions) are caused by the brain and visual systems, and appear to differ from reality. Influenced by objective or psychological factors, observers may register the wrong perceptions of objects in the real world. Illusions vary widely, including perspectival illusions, illusions of distortion, size-constancy illusions, figure–ground illusions, and luminance illusions among others.

The late 16th century Italian illusion paintings *Dignitas Mahvmetana* , by Svperbia Tvrtescha. Two completely different images can be seen when the painting is turned upside down.

Picture/ Wikimedia Commons

In our daily lives, we encounter many visual illusions. For example, afterimages will arise from gazing at the sun for too long time. Viewed from the front, a mountain looks like a range, whereas viewed sideways, it appears to be a peak. Perhaps this is why nowadays, visual illusions have developed into myriads of art forms and applied in many fields.

1. The forced perspective gallery at the Palazzo Spada in Rome by Francesco Borromini, 1632. The 8.6-metre long gallery gives the illusion of being about four times its actual length.
Author/ Livio Andronico
Picture/ Wikimedia Commons

2. Figure afterimage
Author/ Dimitri Parant and Isa Sator
Picture/ Wikimedia Commons

3. Herringbone pattern on the Taj Mahal causes an optic illusion of the pillars' flat surface.
Author/ David Castor
Picture/ Wikimedia Commons

1.

2.

3.

ORIGIN

In ancient times, our ancestors found that a stick would bend when half immerged in water, that ghosting would occur when the eyes peered directly at the sun for a long time, and that rapidly moving objects could lead to motion blur. However, our ancestors could not explain these illusions. At that time visual illusions appeared only in nature.

ANCIENT TIMES

Refraction of light by water-air diopter
Author/ Noé Lecocq
Picture/ Wikimedia Commons

Motion blur of star trails in the Atacama Desert in Chile
Author/ Diana Juncher
Picture/ Wikimedia Commons

A visual illusion in nature: the scene refracted by the water drop inverts reality.
Author/ Marco Verch
Picture/ Wikimedia Commons

An inferior mirage (an optical phenomenon) in the Mojave Desert
Author/ Brocken Inaglory
Picture/ Wikimedia Commons

IN ANCIENT GREECE AND DURING THE MIDDLE AGES

It was not until the 5th century BC that people started to study visual illusion as a phenomenon and try to explain it. Philosophers at that time held two opinions. Epicharmus, an ancient Greek philosopher, believed human senses were not paying enough attention and were "messing up." He is quoted as saying, "The mind sees and the mind hears. The rest is blind and deaf." He thought that even if human minds know and understand everything clearly, the sensory organs deceive the mind and present a visual illusion. However, Protagoras, another ancient Greek philosopher, held a different opinion: that human senses and bodies were fine, but the environment was the one messing up. He said, "Man is nothing but a bundle of sensations." For him, it was the environment that fools us and not the senses.

The debate continued. Another philosopher who became fascinated visual illusion appeared: Plato. Plato believed that the trickery and the reality of visual illusions were due both to the mind and the senses. He then said that the eyes and mind need to work together to create such illusions.

5TH CENTURY BC

Epicharmus believed that the human senses were not paying enough attention and were "messing up."

A portrait of Epicharmus (1828)
Artist/ Giuseppe Emanuele Ortolani
Picture/ Wikimedia Commons

Protagoras held a different opinion: that human senses and bodies were fine, but the environment was the one messing up.

Democritus (center) and Protagoras (right)
(17th century)
Artist/ Salvator Rosa
Picture/ Wikimedia Commons

370 BC

Plato believed that the trickery and reality of visual illusions were due to both the mind and the senses.

Plato (370 BC)
Picture/ Wikimedia Commons

Aristotle, who lived around 350 BC, said that Epicharmus and Protagoras were both right and wrong. He reasoned that human senses can be trusted, but that they can also be easily fooled. For example, on hot days standing near a road, you can observe heat waves rising. Your senses are right, you can see the waves. But, if you look through the waves, at a tree, the tree, falsely, appears to be wiggling.

350 BC

Aristotle reasoned that human senses can be trusted, but they can also be easily misled.

Bust of Aristotle

As knowledge about visual illusion increased, artists began to apply it to architecture and paintings, and a number of outstanding artists and artworks emerged. The most famous examples are the architecture of the Parthenon in Ancient Greece and all varieties of perspective paintings and illusion paintings in the Middle Ages.

438 BC

The Parthenon in Athens, Greece, built in 447 BC-438 BC

The architect overcame the size difference between the tops and bottoms of the columns by using parallel protrusions. These made the size of the upper and lower columns appear to be the same.

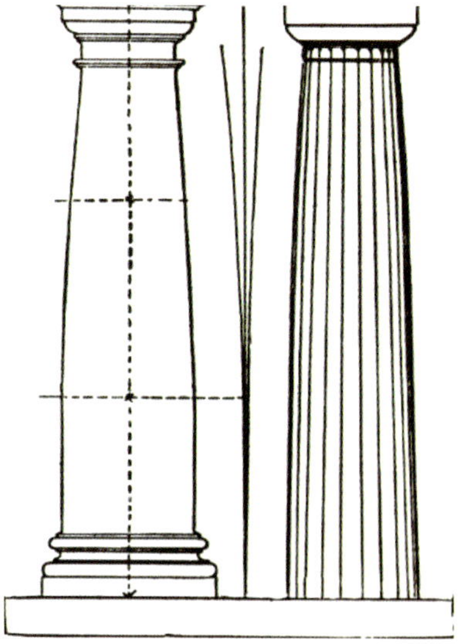

IN MODERN TIMES

With the development of psychology and physics, a deeper, more comprehensive understanding of visual illusion emerged.
In the 19th century, Johannes Peter Müller, a psychologist, and J.J. Oppel, a German high-school teacher, performed various studies related to how people perceive visual illusions. Articles they wrote reignited public interest in the phenomenon.

15TH CENTURY

Upward foreshortening was used in the frescoes at Loreto, Italy.
Artist/ Melozzo da Forlì

Perspective was used in this fresco at the Sistine Chapel.
Artist/ Pietro Perugino

Linear perspective was adapted in the painting *The Last Supper*.
Artist/ Leonardo da Vinci

19TH CENTURY

Müller stated the underlying principle of illusions between the nervous action and the mechanism of the senses. He argued that sensation following stimulation of a sensory nerve does not depend on the mode of stimulation but upon the nature of the sense organ. Thus light, pressure, or mechanical stimulation acting on the retina and optic nerve invariably produce luminous impressions. However, few people knew what he was talking about at that time because he was the first person to call distortions visual illusions.

Johannes Peter Müller

Pictures/ Wikimedia Commons

In 1854, J.J. Oppel argued that when an illusion involves properties that fall within the purview of geometry, it is geometrical-optical. This means that visual illusions can be categorized according to the nature of the differences between objects and percepts. For example, these differences can include differences in brightness, color, location, size, orientation, and depth.
The research of Johannes Peter Müller and J.J. Oppel played a very significant role in the development of visual or optical illusions.

1854

J.J. Oppel argued that when an illusion involves properties that fall within the purview of geometry, it is geometrical-optical.

1860

Geometrical-optical illusions

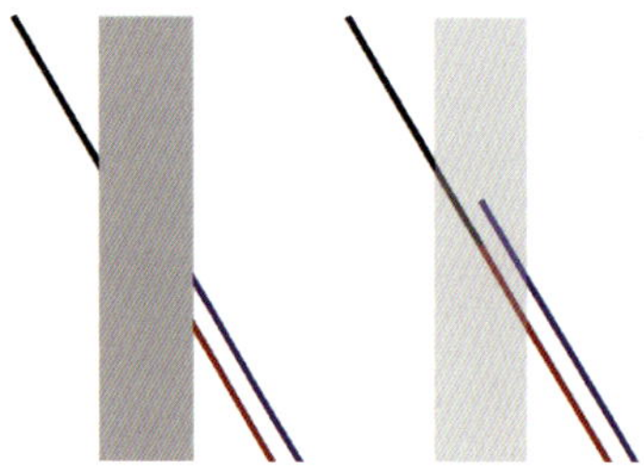

The Poggendorff Illusion
The black line and red line are obscured by a grey rectangle. The blue line, rather than the red line, appears to be a continuation of the black one, which is clearly shown not to be the case in the second picture. Instead there is an apparent position shift of the lower portion of the line.

The Zöllner Illusion
A series of parallel, black diagonal lines are crossed with short, repeating lines. The direction of the crossing lines alternates between horizontal and vertical, which creates the illusion that the black lines are not parallel.

1865

Mach Bands
Mach bands are optical illusions observed in an image consisting of different shades of gray. The human eye perceives two narrow stripes of different gradients of luminosity at each border. These are not present in the true image, and increase the contrast between the areas.

Afterwards, Hermann von Helmholtz, a physicist from Germany, put forth the idea of cognitive illusion. He agreed with Protagoras. According to Protagoras, the assumptions people hold about their environment trigger cognitive illusion. The human brain and eyes make unconscious inferences based on these assumptions and thereby create cognitive illusions. The café wall illusion is the best example of cognitive illusion. Black and white colors cross together to break the parallelism between lines, resulting the line's curvature in human vision.

In 1915 illustrator W.E. Hill developed a cartoon of a young lady and an old woman merged together, which is another perfect example of visual illusion. Some people saw an old woman whereas others saw a young lady. Due to different individual perceptions,people can see different images in the cartoon. Watching the sketch carefully reveals that different images are merged together skillfully. This type of illusion paintings appeared in various fields in the past few centuries.

1821

1894

Hermann von Helmholtz put forth the idea of cognitive illusion.

Hermann von Helmholtz
Picture/ Wikimedia Commons

The café wall illusion: the horizontal lines are parallel, despite appearing to jut off different angles from each other.

The Port 1010, building inspired by the café wall illusion, in the Docklands region of Melbourne, Australia.

Photographer/ Joe Bekker
Picture/ Wikimedia Commons

1915

My Wife and My Mother in *Law in Puck* magazine
Artist/ W. E. Hill
Picture/ Wikimedia Commons

THE RISE OF OP ART ——

Op art, short for optical art, is a style of visual art that uses optical illusions. Op art works are abstract, with better-known pieces created in black and white. Typically, they give the viewer the impression of movement, hidden images, flashing and vibrating patterns, or of swelling or warping.

Op art is a perceptual experience related to how vision functions. It is a dynamic visual art that stems from a discordant figure-ground relationship that places the two planes—foreground and background in a tense and contradictory juxtaposition. There are two main methods of operation to create Op art works: (a) the figure-ground relationship and (b) color interaction.

The first, the figure-ground relationship, is the best-known method: creating effects through pattern and line. Often these paintings are black and white, or grisaille. Here, black and white wavy lines are close to one another on the canvas surface, creating a volatile figure-ground relationship.

1960S

1959-1961

Supernovae in the Tate Modern, London, in which the arrangement of black and white dots produces a flickering effect in the image.
Artist/ Victor Vasarely
Photographer/ Mramoeba

Wild Cats
Author/ Nevit Dilmen

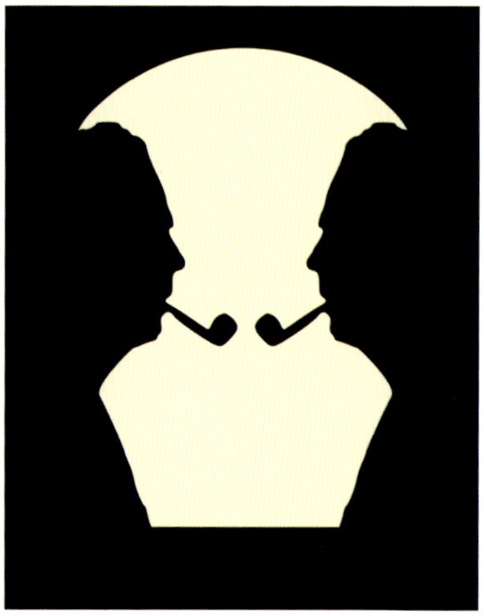

Mr. Pipo's Face or Vase
Author/ Nevit Dilmen

The second example, famous Italian optical-kinetic artist Getulio Alviani employs color interaction. He treated aluminum surfaces to create vibrating light patterns that change as the observer moves.
What's more, the afterimages of certain colors will occur in lines due to the way the retina receives and processes light. Artists take advantage of this phenomenon to make colors interact.

Since 1965, artists have produced color-based Op art. They have created dynamic visual effects by arranging sets of lines, dots, and patterns. The dynamic effect usually occurs on the fringe of two colors strongly contrasting in hue yet very close in brightness. Red is the color most likely to create a dynamic effect because of its brightness and lightness. Often, artists need to focus on the dynamic effects between the graphics and the background while paying attention to another element: contrasting colors that have different effects on the eyes.

Soto Sphere at the Jesús Soto Museum of Modern Art. The artist used vertical lines and colors to create a circle that does not actually exist.
Artist/ Jesús Rafael Soto
Photographer/ Guillermo Ramos Flamerich

Title/ *Cosmic Voyage*
Artist/ Henrique José Teixeira Matos

Title/ *Optical Motion*
Artist/ Henrique José Teixeira Matos

Title/ *Travel to Infinity*
Artist/ Henrique José Teixeira Matos

Pictures/ Wikimedia Commons

AT PRESENT

Nowadays a number of excellent contemporary artists of visual illusion—such as Shigeo Fukuda, Rob Gonsalves, Patrick Hughes, and Akiyoshi Kitaoka—have used visual illusion in various fields such as painting, graphic design, 3-D painting, anamorphic art, advertising, packaging, architecture, and urban public space.

THE CONTEMPORARY DEVELOPMENT OF VISUAL ILLUSION

2007

Artist used refraction to form a complete picture on the round tube.

Artist/ István Orosz Photographer/ YY Photo/ Wikimedia Commons

The Floor of Casa-Museo Concha Piquer de Valencia
The designer combined lines and colors to make the floor look three-dimensional.
Author/ Daniel Villafruela
Photo/ Wikimedia Commons

2017

When the viewer moves his or her body to the side or up and down, patterns in the picture seem to be convex forward.

Title/ Wooden It Be Possible
Artist/ Patrick Hughes

An optical illusion similar to *Rotating Snakes* by Kitaoka Akiyoshi. Color interaction and the arrangement of circles were used to create the rolling illusion.
Author/ Cmglee
Picture/ Wikimedia Commons

2

CREATIONS OF VISUAL ILLUSIONS

The first chapter shows us the interesting history of visual illusion. However, what is the cause of visual illusion? How do we create illusion pictures? What are the mysterious principles of different classic illusion images? Based on science, this chapter will reveal the mystery of visual illusion for you.

THE FORMATION OF VISUAL ILLUSION

▶ ILLUSION CAUSED BY THE OBJECT ITSELF

Some illusions are produced by placing together a collection of images. Each individual image may be easily seen, but the images, when all combined together, may appear unrecognizably different than when viewed separately, as in the originals.

While viewing a visual illusion, one may see two very different images when focusing first on the whole image, and then second on the smaller details of the image.

▲ Vertumnus ,the Roman God of the seasons

Artist/ Giuseppe Arcimboldo (1527--1593) Picture/ Wikimedia Commons

▲ The Lawyer

▼ The Librarian

▲ Four Seasons in One Head

Artist/ Giuseppe Arcimboldo (1527--1593) Picture/ Wikimedia Commons

▶ THE PHYSIOLOGICAL FACTOR

Vision is the result of eyes and brain working together. When the information from the eyes deceives the brain, making it see an unreal image, visual illusion occurs.
The light emitted by the outside world passes through the cornea and enters the eyes from the pupil, stimulating the photoreceptor cells on the retina. The nerve impulse generated by the photoreceptor cells enters the visual cortex of the cerebral cortex , along the optic nerve. Finally the scene in the brain is formed. This "scene" is the result of brain processing.

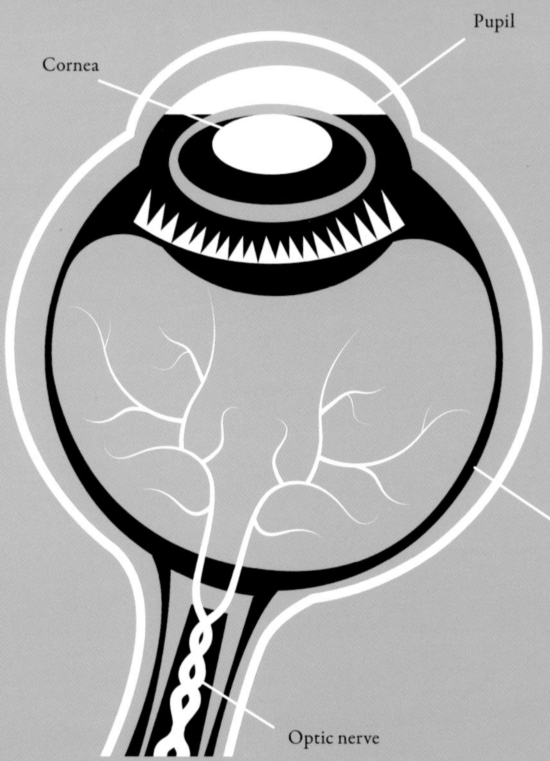

Diagram of Human Eye

When the eyes send visual information to the brain, the brain chooses which parts to focus on. Depending on the focus, different layers of the image may be seen. Some repeated images may even make the visual system overload, thus creating a physiological illusion.

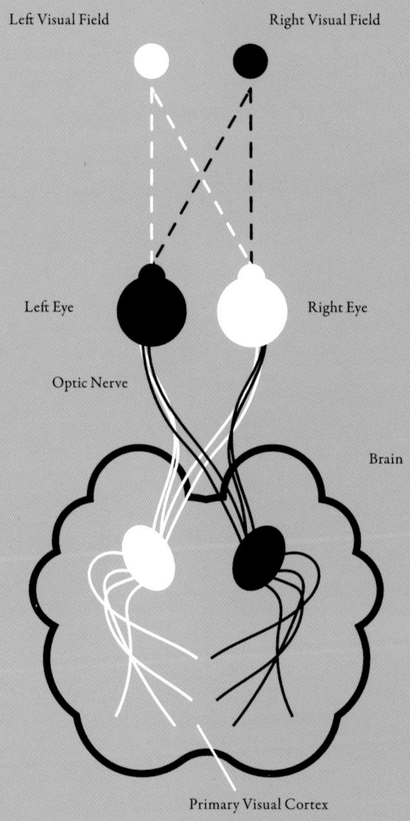

Visual Transmission

1.

2.

1.The Hermann Grid Illusion
The image is made of black squares and white lines. When looking at it, you will likely see faint black dots where the white lines cross.

2.The unmovable image deceives the visual system with distorted lines, making it seem to be rotating.

3.The Scintillating-Grid Illusion
Dark dots seem to appear and disappear rapidly at random intersections. The repeated grid makes the brain overload. When a person keeps his or her eyes directly on a single intersection, the dark dot does not appear. The dark dots disappear if one is too close to or too far from the image.

3.

▶ THE PSYCHOLOGICAL FACTOR

Psychology exercises a variety of effects on the "visual illusion" phenomenon. The most common is the impact of psychological hints and cognitive experiences on the information received by the eyes. For example, when experiencing insomnia or pain, we may feel that time moves slowly. Looking at red, yellow, and orange, however, we may feel warm and passionate. Seeing sharp items, people feel painful and the scalp becomes numb. Obviously, perceptions of objects are always affected by psychological emotions or past experiences. Based on past experiences, the brain will automatically fill in the missing information, and sometimes it is even different from the real situation.

Kanizsa's Triangle
These spatially separate fragments give the impression of a triangle in the middle, which does not exist. The brain automatically fills it in.

Most cognitive illusions occur when some changes have taken place in the objective environment, but people still make judgments in the original modes of perception. Meanwhile, illusions are also the result of various sensations interacting with one another.

A Size-Constancy Illusion
According to our experience, an object far away from us looks smaller than when it is close to us. Thus, even though the two circles in the image are the same size, the brain believes that the back ground circle looks larger.

PRINCIPLES OF VISUAL ILLUSIONS

POSITION RELATIONSHIP

Lines converging toward one point provide perspective. When placing the same-size objects on different positions along the lines, the object closest to the concentration point will seem larger.

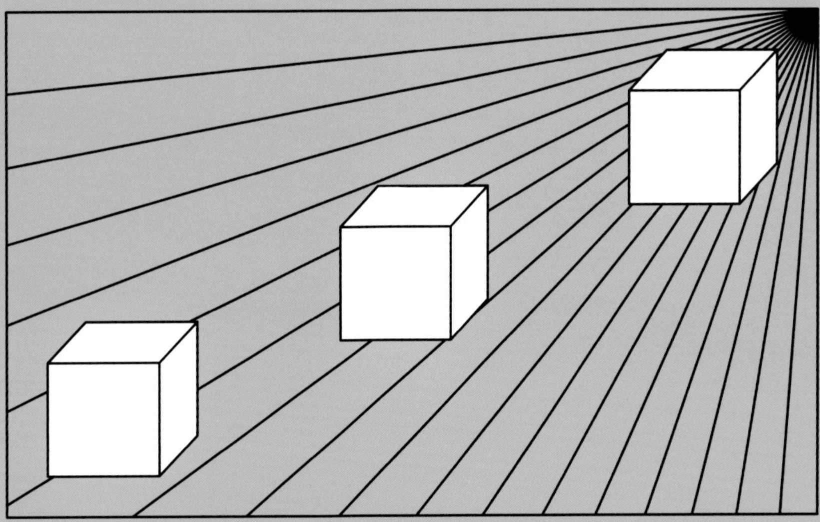

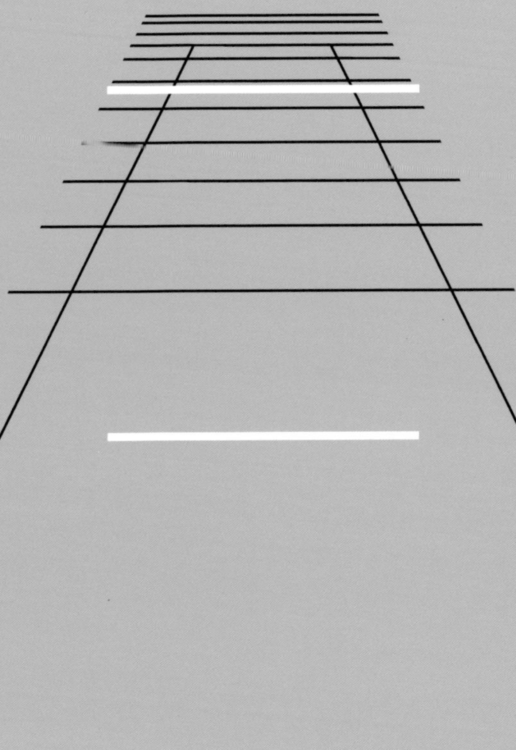

Ponzo Illusion

RELATIVE SIZE

Two circles of identical size are surrounded by large circles and small circles respectively. The central circle surrounded by large circles appears smaller than the one surrounded by small circles. However, there is not always a correlation between the size of the surrounding shapes or the relative size of the central shape. Sarcone's Crosses have proved that among three crosses of the same size, the one surrounded by large squares appears larger instead of smaller.

Ebbinghaus Illusion

Sarcone's Crosses

POSITION SHIFT ILLUSION

Dislocation will happen when a line is cut off by two parallel lines or a plane.

The Poggendorff Illusion

MORPHOLOGICAL DEFORMATION

Intersected by external lines from different directions and of different numbers and forms, straight lines seem distorted whereas parallel lines seem non-parallel.

The Hering Illusion
Lines are emitted from a point between two parallel lines, causing the parallel lines to bend outward.

The Wundt Illusion
Lines are emitted from two points on both sides of two parallel lines, causing the parallel lines to bend inward.

COLOR CONTRAST

Placing together two inversely black-and-white shapes of the same size, observers will feel that the size of the white shape is larger. In other words, when size is equal, the whiter it is, the larger the shape appears. On the contrary, the less white it is, the smaller the shape will appear to be.

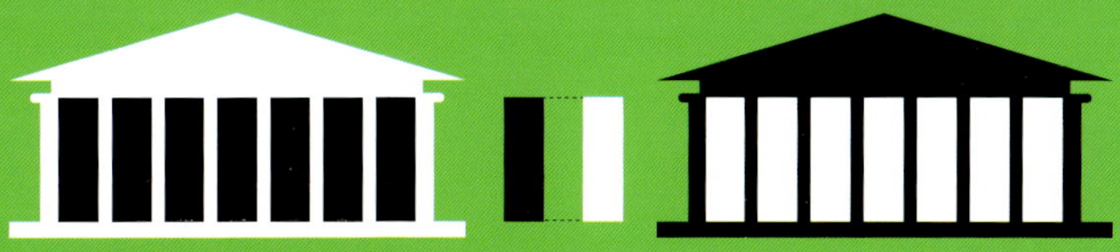

BACKGROUND DIFFERENCES

The hue of a color will apparently change due to the alteration of the color of the background. For example, the color will seem lighter while combined with white, and darker when combined with the black.

The Bezold Effect

Chubb Illusion

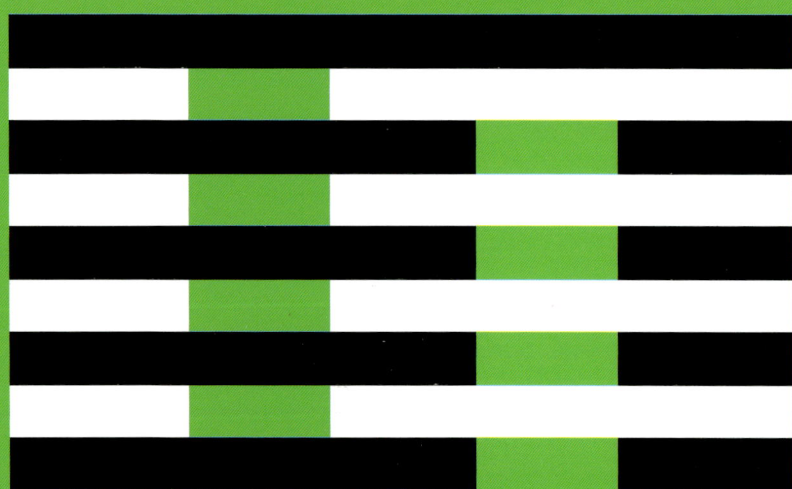

White's Illusion

EDGE PERCEPTION

Sensory perception of edges can be evoked by changing the arrangement of lines or graphics or by connecting the various components of the graphics to form a complete image. Then people will see non-existent, illusory contours.

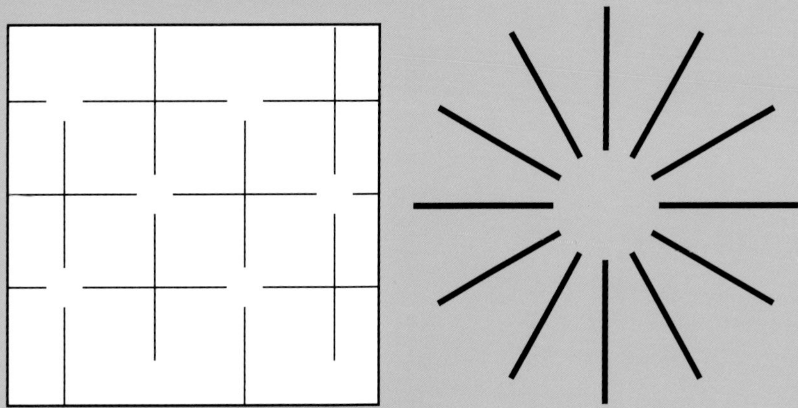

The Ehrenstein Illusion

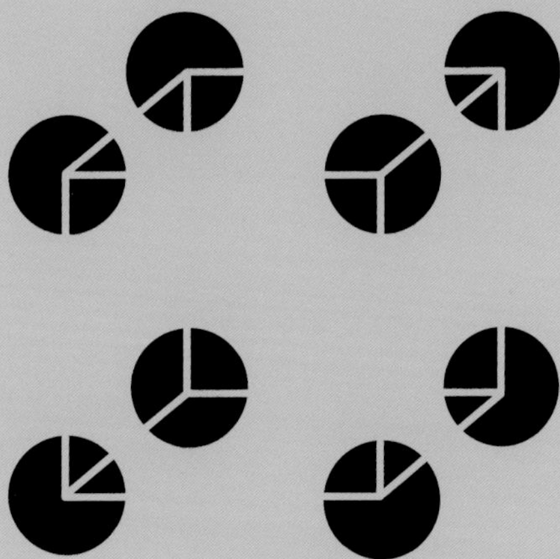

FIGURE PERCEPTION

When black-and-white wavy lines are close to one another on the canvas surface, they create a volatile figure. The perceived figure depends on the direction to which the border between the black-and-white regions is assigned.

Rubin's Vase

SPIRAL ILLUSION

A sequence of tilted elements caused by overlapping concentric circles makes the eyes feel the distortion of illusion and see a spiral.

Fraser Spiral Illusion

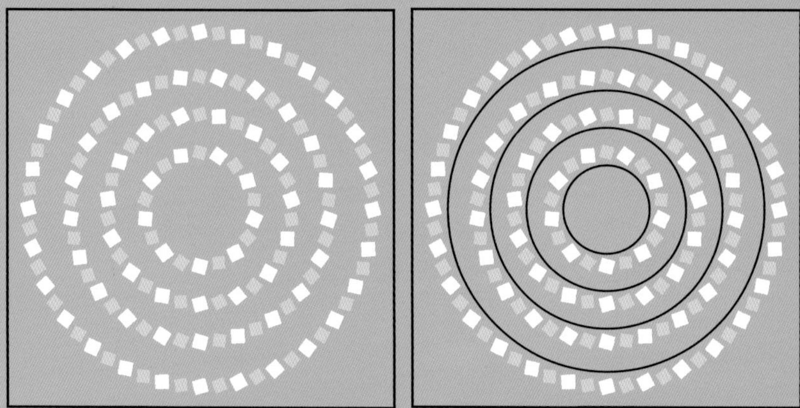

Pinna's Illusory Intertwining Effect

VERTICAL–HORIZONTAL ILLUSION

The vertical line will appear to be longer than the horizontal line, though they are the same length.

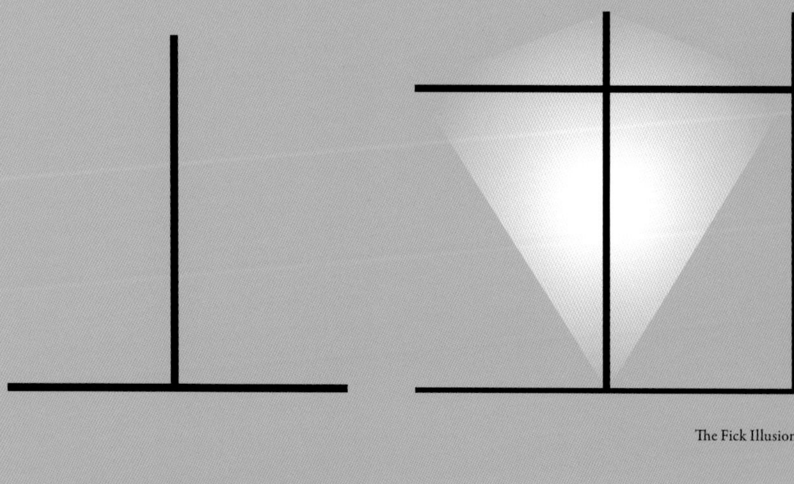

The Fick Illusion

DIRECTION RELATIONSHIP

The visual system's process for judging depth and distance usually assumes that the "angles-in" configuration corresponds to an object that is closer, making it appear larger or longer, and that the "angles-out" configuration corresponds to an object far away, making it appear smaller or shorter.

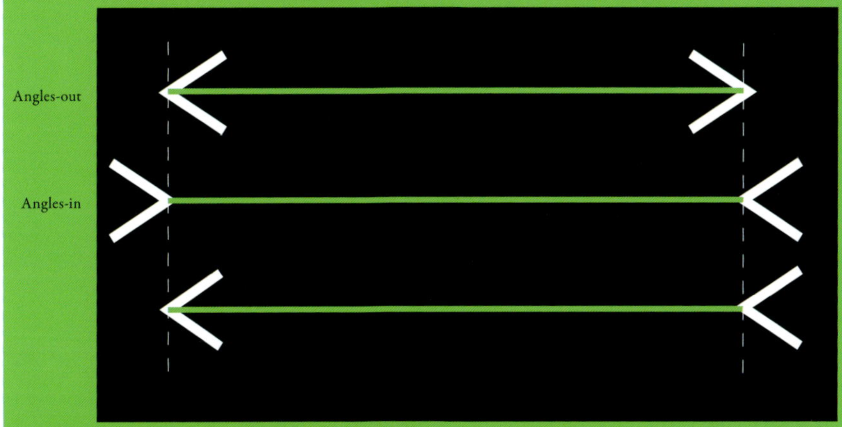

The Müller Lyer Illusion

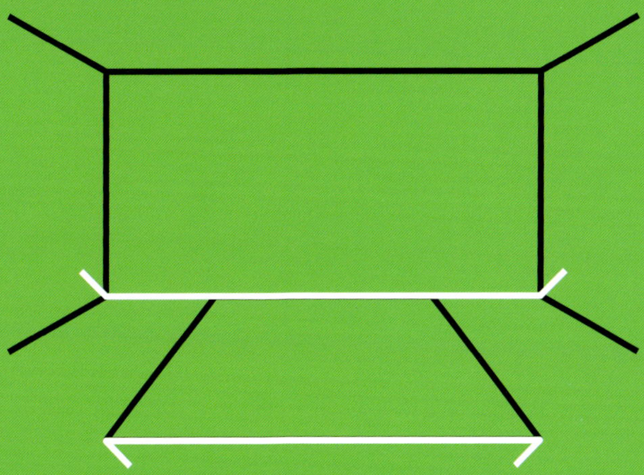

THE SHADOW ILLUSION

Shadowing the image in which color is regular in light and dark, even if the squares of the same color will look different in tones.

Checker Shadow Illusion
In these two images, the checkerboards are filled with light checks and dark checks regularly. Thus, the colors of Zone A and Zone B should be different. However, by adding shadow on Zone B, the colors of Zone A and Zone B become the same. Yet our eyes still believe that they are in two different color tones because of conventional thinking.

THE TILT ILLUSION

Because of a spatial context, the perceived orientation of a line or grating pattern can appear tilted away from its physical orientation.

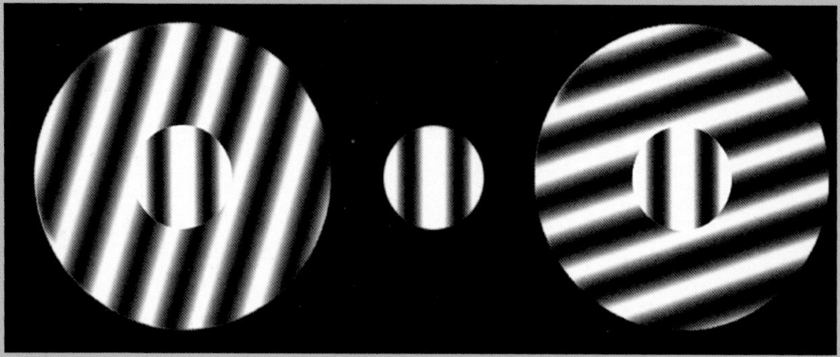

Affected by peripheral lines, the vertical lines in the inner circle seem to be tilted to the left.

THE PERIPHERAL DRIFT ILLUSION

When luminance grating appears in the visual periphery, temporal differences in the luminance processing of the eyes will produce a signal that tricks the motion system and the motion illusion appears.

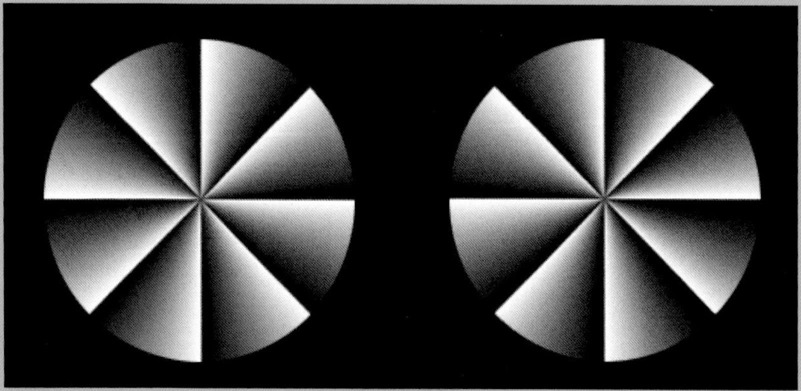

INSTRUCTION MANUAL OF GRAPHIC ILLUSIONS

Nowadays, there are various kinds of optical illusion artworks and graphic designs which seem complicated and changeable. However, the principle of each work is traceable. This chapter features different types of optical illusion artworks from around the world and presents their process of creation in a simple and intuitive way. You can also do it by yourself!

3

POSITIVE SPACE AND NEGATIVE SPACE

Positive space and negative space in graphic design are transformed in the figure-ground relationship.
It is an artistic image that can show people an illusion and make them see two different images.

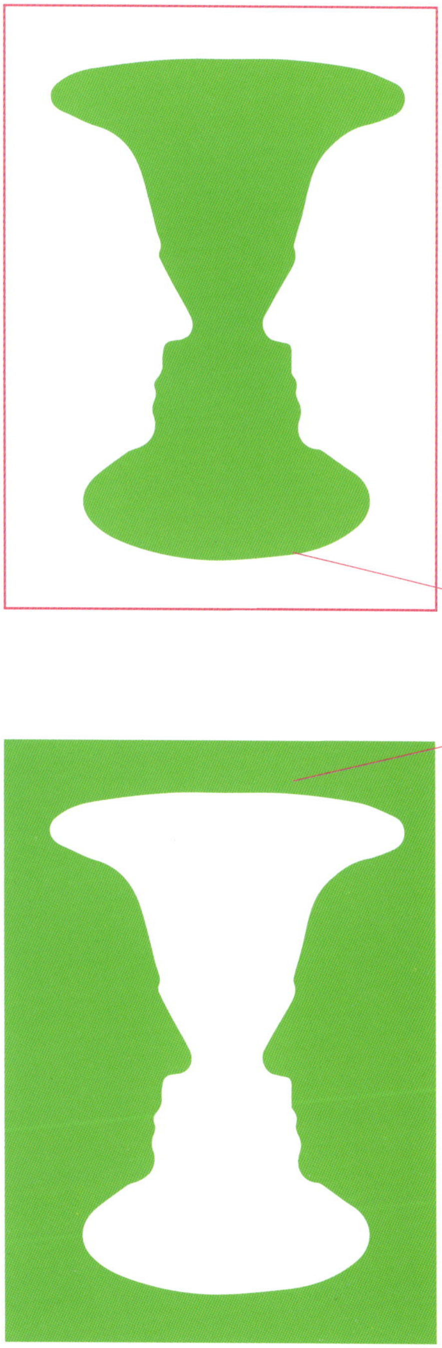

1. The figure and ground can be transformed.

2. The boundary of two patterns is shared.

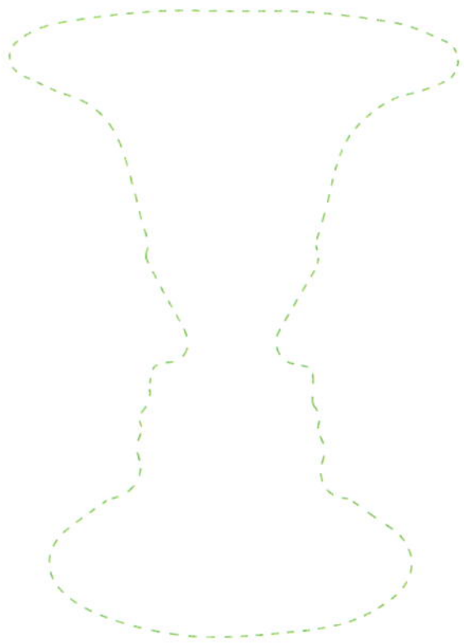

3. The overall structure is balanced.

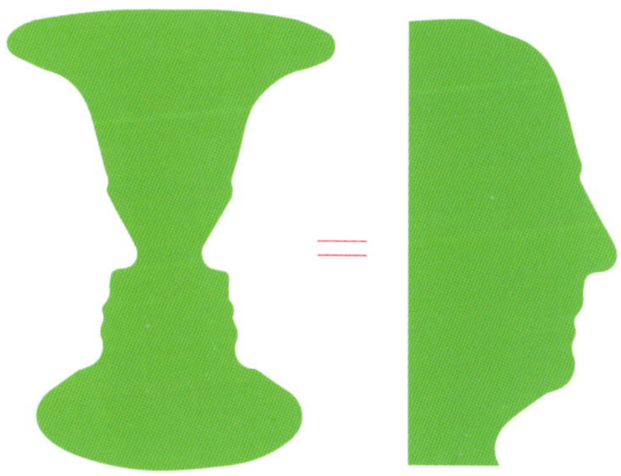

DO IT YOURSELF!

What can you get from the figure and the ground?

Mumbai is a city crowded not just with people but also many stray animals, which are neglected and are often perceived as being a nuisance. In this fast-paced city, people always complain about lack of time or space. To inspire co-existence between stray animals and the people of Mumbai, World for All developed a pet-adoption campaign to inspire compassion for strays.

WORLD FOR ALL: A BEAUTIFUL PET-ADOPTION CAMPAIGN

Design: McCann   Creative Director: Pranav Bhide

While designing the campaign poster, Pranav Bhide cleverly used negative space to capture these striking optical illusions: silhouettes of animals such as puppy, kitten, and rabbit can be seen between the people, proving that there is always room for a pet in our lives and urging people to adopt rather than simply adapt.

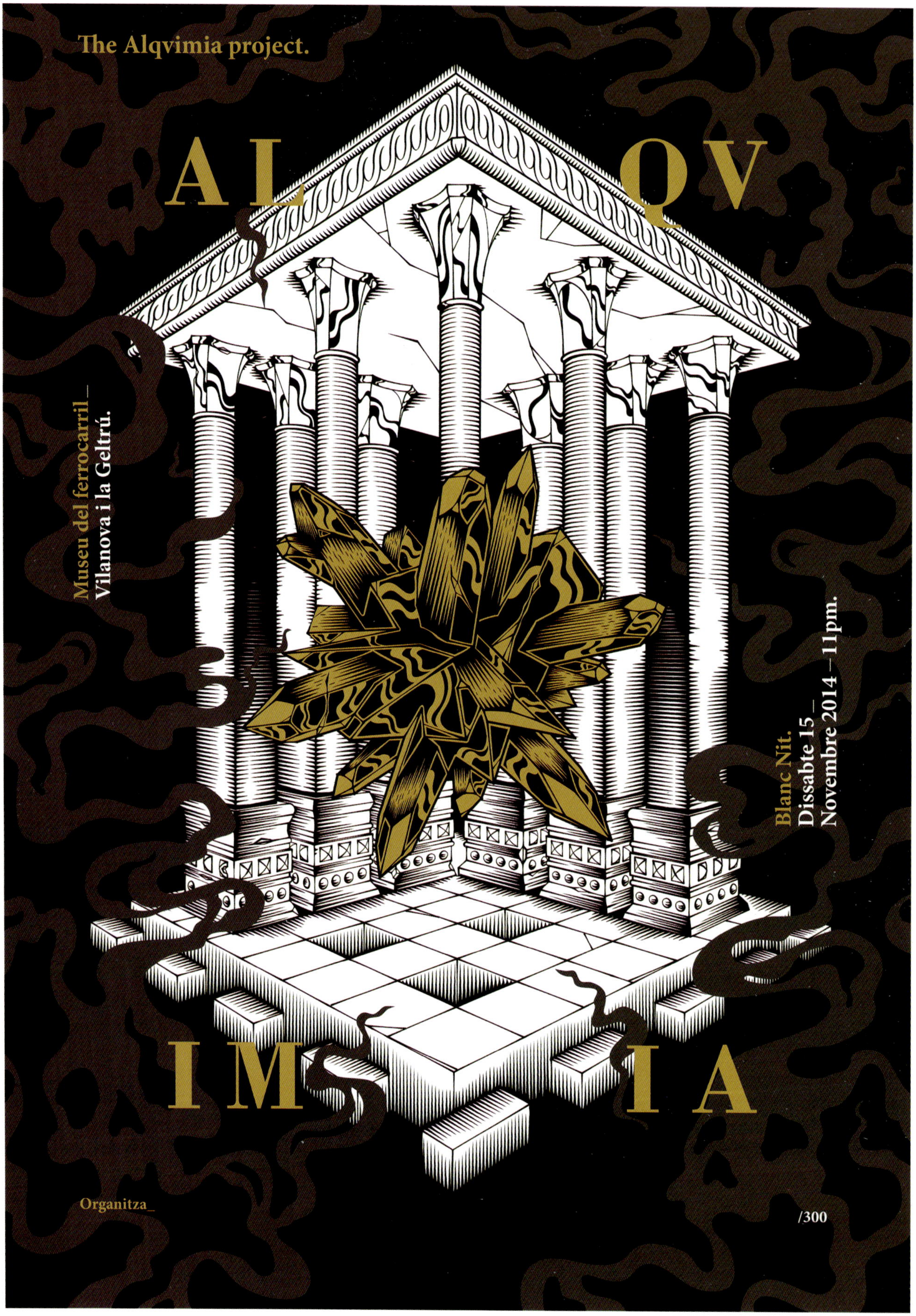

ALQUIMIA _ BLANCNIT

Design: Pedro Baños, Adrià Molins, Sergi Delgado, Oscar Medina

The Alquimia project is a poster for the Blanc Festival, a graphic design festival based in Barcelona. It is a proposal based on new creative techniques, including video-mapping, interactive design, etc. It is also an innovation in the field of illusion geometry and surrealistic op art.

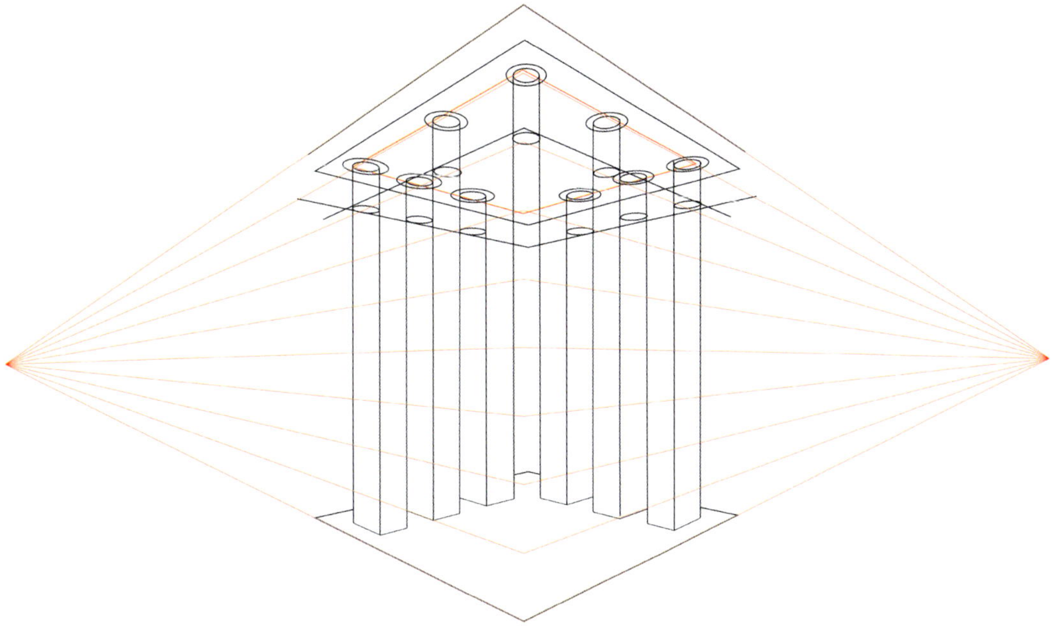

Focusing on the top, viewers can see that the round columns are arranged around the four sides of the roof. However, while looking down, viewers see that the round columns gradually change into square columns and that their position is changed to the two sides of the floor.

Using the mesmerizing and powerful art of negative space, the designer attempts to convey the impressions that the Land Rover is not just about off-road driving but embodies a comprehensive lifestyle.

Employing a clever and simple visual effect, these posters, buildings, and skyscrapers are gradually transformed into defoliating trees, a forest, and a waterfall: which suggests that the Land Rover is good for driving both in field and city.

LANDROVER FREELANDER

Design: Tang Yau Hoong

LAND ROVER

LAND
ROVER

LAND
ROVER

Journey to the City of No Horizon

Light Painter

PERSONAL ILLUSTRATIONS

These surrealistic personal illustrations were created using negative space. Thus the illustrator tells stories of the river and sky (Journey to the City of No Horizon), of paint and light (Light Painter), and of a city and light bulbs (The Hanging City).

Design: Tang Yau Hoong

▲ The Hanging City

Graphic designer Levente Szabo specializes in the use of positive and negative spaces.

For cover designed for Linda Coggin's novel *The Boy with the Tiger's Heart*, he combined woods and sunset, employing the silhouettes of trees as positive space and the shape of tiger created by the shadow of the trees and sunset in the background as negative space. This creates a magical scene where people, tiger, and nature coexist. At the same time, it hints at the theme of this book—the call of the wild.

THE BOY WITH THE TIGER'S HEART

Design: Levente Szabo

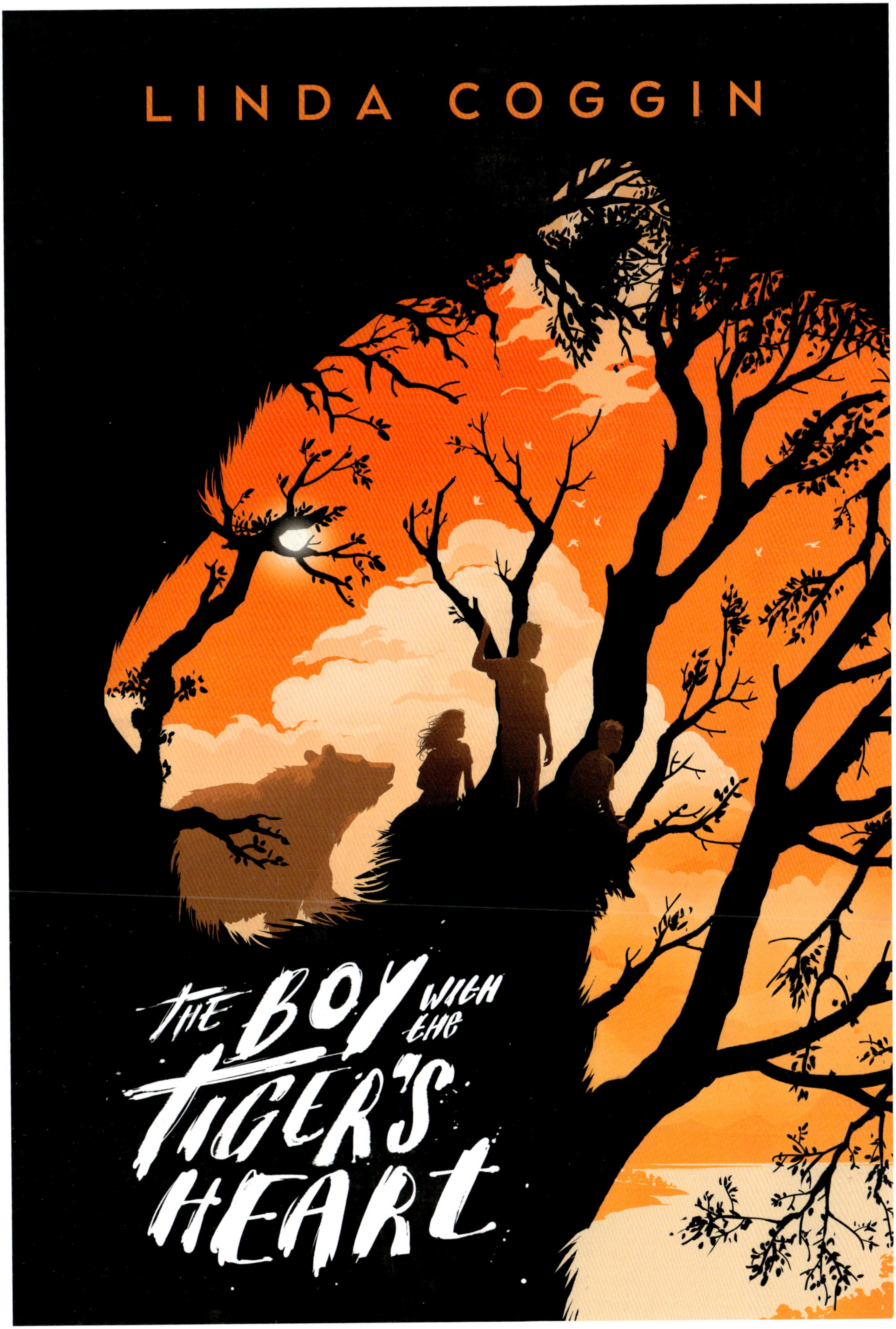
LINDA COGGIN
THE BOY WITH THE TIGER'S HEART

When designing other book covers, Levente Szabo created fantastic and unique images by assigning smoke and a face, the contours of a house and the devil, as the positive and negative spaces.

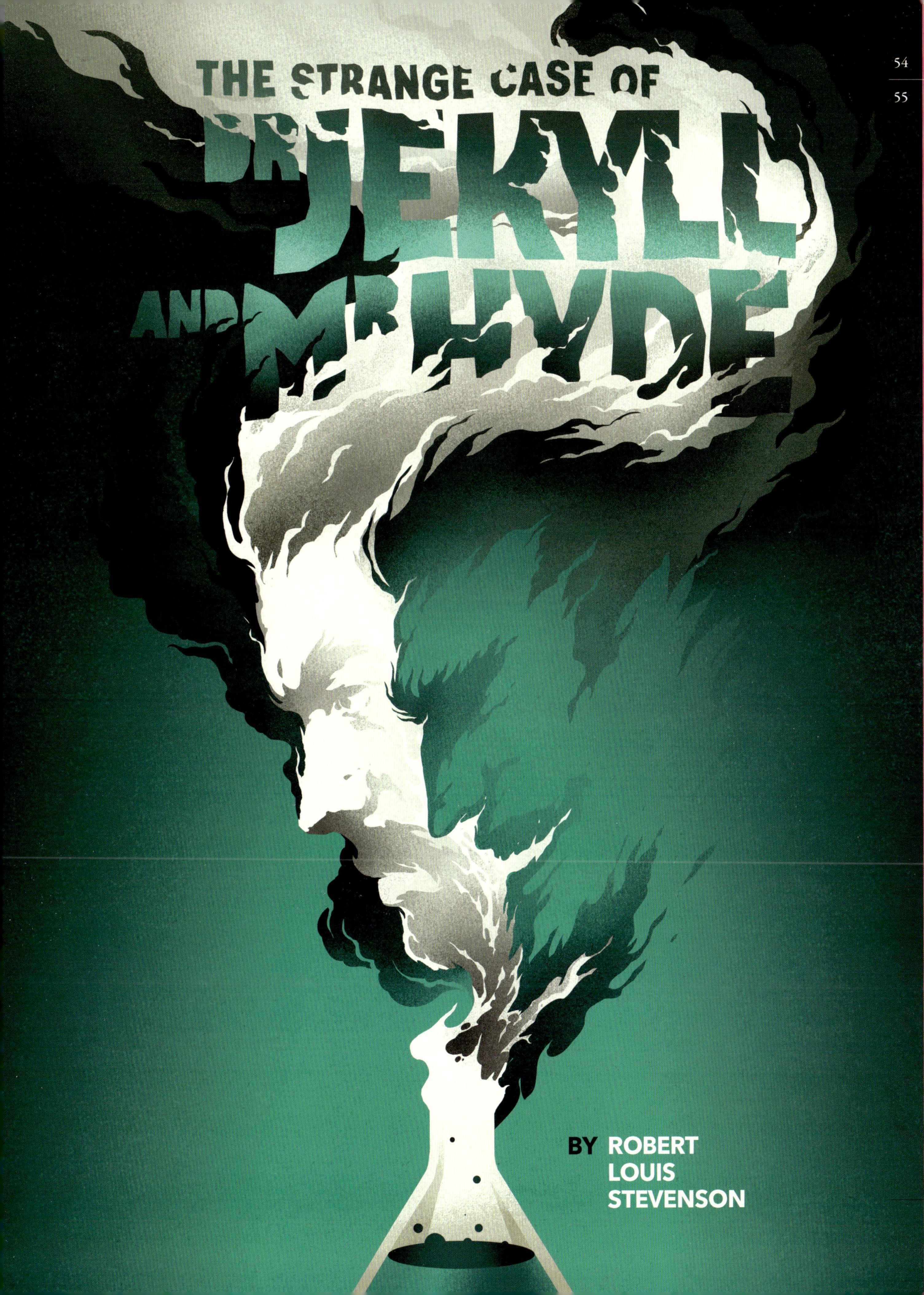
THE STRANGE CASE OF
DR JEKYLL
AND MR HYDE
BY ROBERT
LOUIS
STEVENSON

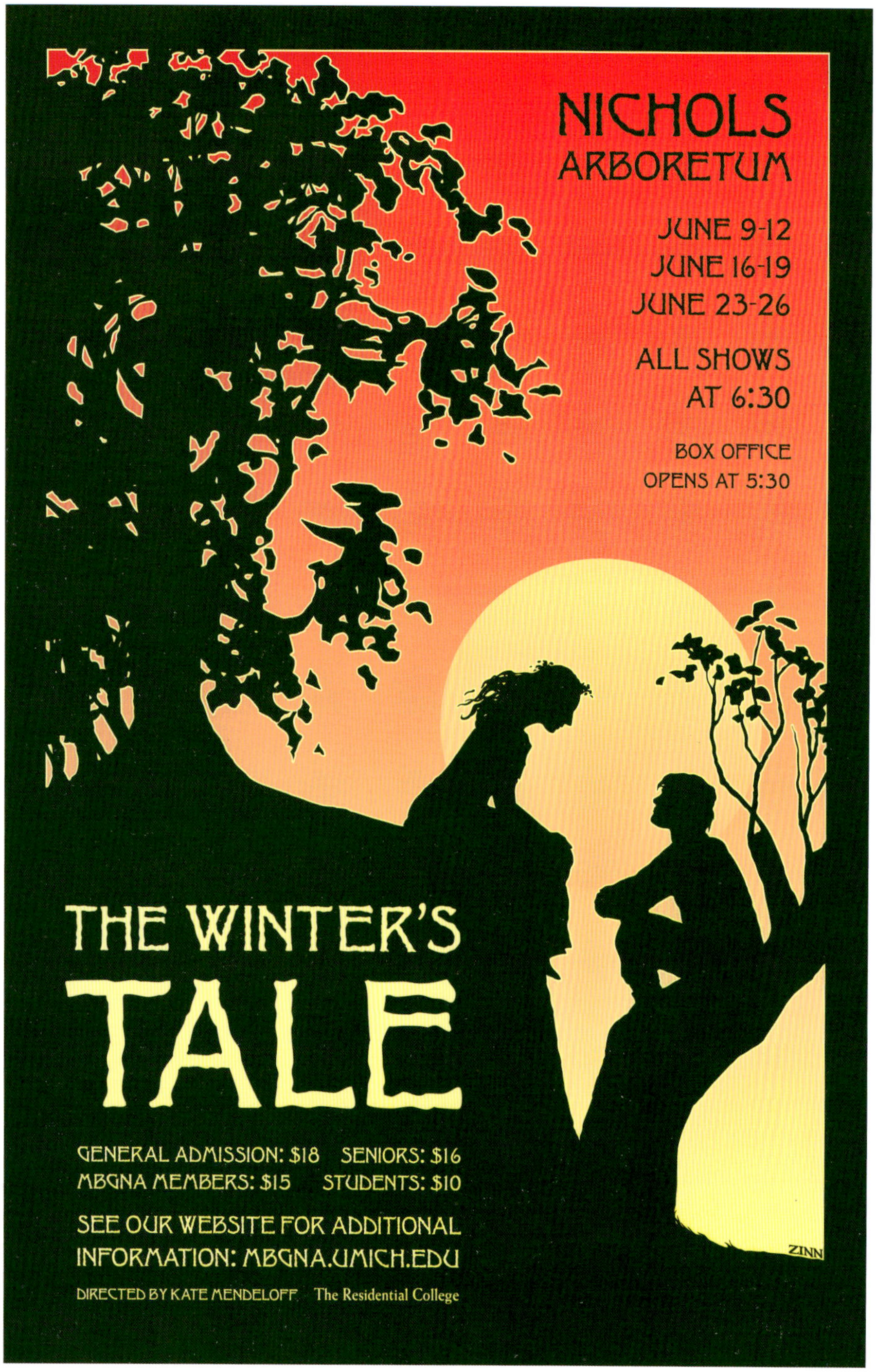

While designing this series of theatrical posters, the artist took advantage of perceptions that lead to unique images. These posters were designed to create a double meaning within the shapes of trees in the positive space and the shape of a human in the negative spaces of the silhouette. This represents the core themes and the human relationships of the story in the latter and the natural outdoor environment in the former.

SHAKESPEARE IN THE ARB

Design: David Zinn

NIGHT
U WILL
ZINN
, 25-28 · ALL SHOWS AT 6:30
MEMBERS: $15 STUDENTS: $10
RECTED BY KATE MENDELOFF The Residential College

SHAKESPEARE IN THE ARB 2012
the MERRY WIVES of
WINDSOR
ZINN
U-M NICHOLS ARBORETUM JUNE 7-10, 14-17 and 21-24
UNIVERSITY OF MICHIGAN
Matthaei Botanical gardens
and Nichols arboretum
DIRECTED BY KATE MENDELOFF, U-M RESIDENTIAL COLLEGE
Shows start 6:30 pm. For ticket and box office information,
visit mbgna.umich.edu or call 734.647.7600.

1

This project includes a series of double images.

The designer combined all the elements together: landscape, animals, people, and plants. The figures represented in the primary plane were carefully arranged in such a manner that they formed a human face in the secondary plane.

DUOSCOPIC SELF-PORTRAIT

Artist : Josean Figueroa

2

3

1.Dobleautore Tratocubom Etafisico
2.Autobodegon
3.Cubometafisico13

Autoretrato Duoscopico

Freud/St.George

1 CUBOMETAFISICO6-2007

2 APARICION4ANGEL2b-2007

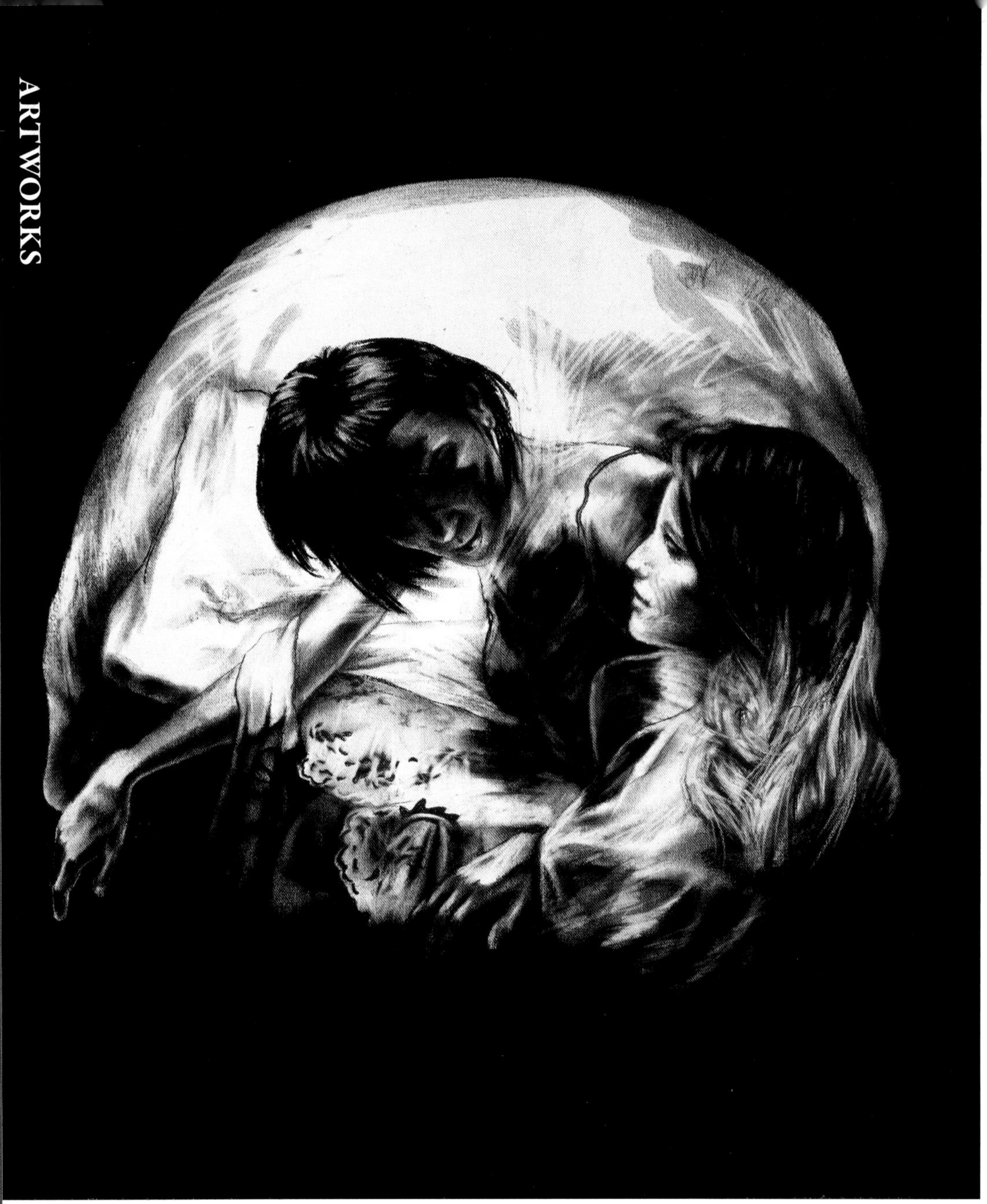

Tom French's paintings offer a visual discourse on dualism. His concerns with physical and metaphysical duality are reflected in the double images of his artworks: in which faces, figures, and skulls repeat and shadow one another.
When viewing these pieces, the first thing seen is the image of a skull. Then, as the viewer approaches the work and takes a closer look, formerly hidden figures will appear.

DUALITIES

Design: Tom French

This transformation from a dark skull (the symbol of death) to the female form (the representation of beauty, vitality, and fertility) brings a dead object to life by humanizing it. The closer people get to the image, the more alive it comes.

French chooses a monochrome palette and charcoal to draw these paintings, the simplicity of which allows for the play of light and dark to expand in unexpectedly haunting ways.

French thinks that each scene in his paintings offers a snapshot of a story: with a dynamic between the characters on various levels that ties into the larger picture. There is much more to these images than illusion alone.

THE IMPOSSIBLE OBJECTS

1 Impossible Cube

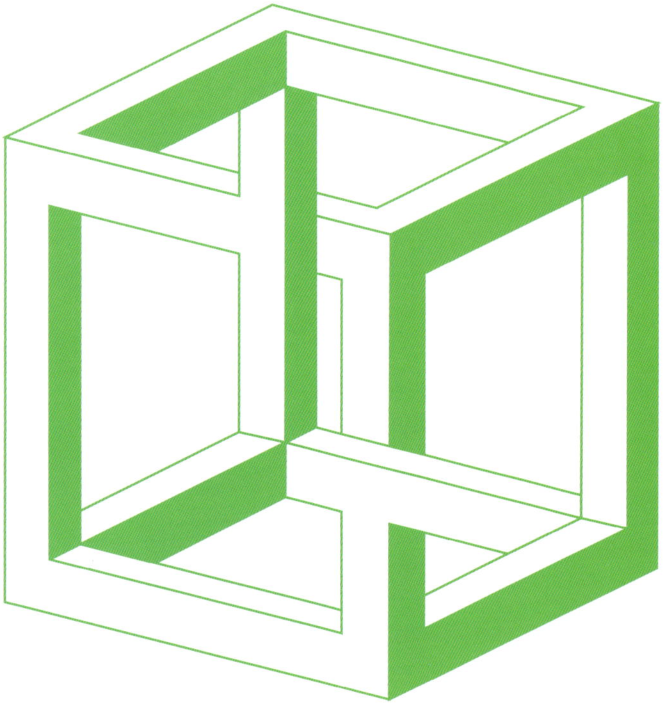

The Impossible Cube was designed by M.C. Escher for his artwork ***Belvedere***. Simply, in this cube, one of its edges which should be closer to the observer, is covered by another edge, which should be farther from the observer. Thus, the illusion is created, which portrays a cube impossible in the real world.

2 Penrose Triangle

The Penrose Triangle was first created by the Swedish artist Oscar Reutersvärd and then promoted by the mathematician Roger Penrose in the 1950s. It is characterized by the fact that the triangle is distorted to the shapes which are unavailable physically. The similar figures include Penrose Square, Penrose Pentagon, etc.

3 Penrose Stairs

The Penrose Stairs is an impossible object created by Lionel Penrose and his son Roger Penrose. A variation on the Penrose Triangle, it is a two-dimensional depiction of a staircase in which the stairs make four 90-degree turns as they ascend or descend yet form a continuous loop, so that a person could climb it forever and never get any higher. This is clearly impossible in three-dimensional space.[1]

4 Devil's Tuning Fork

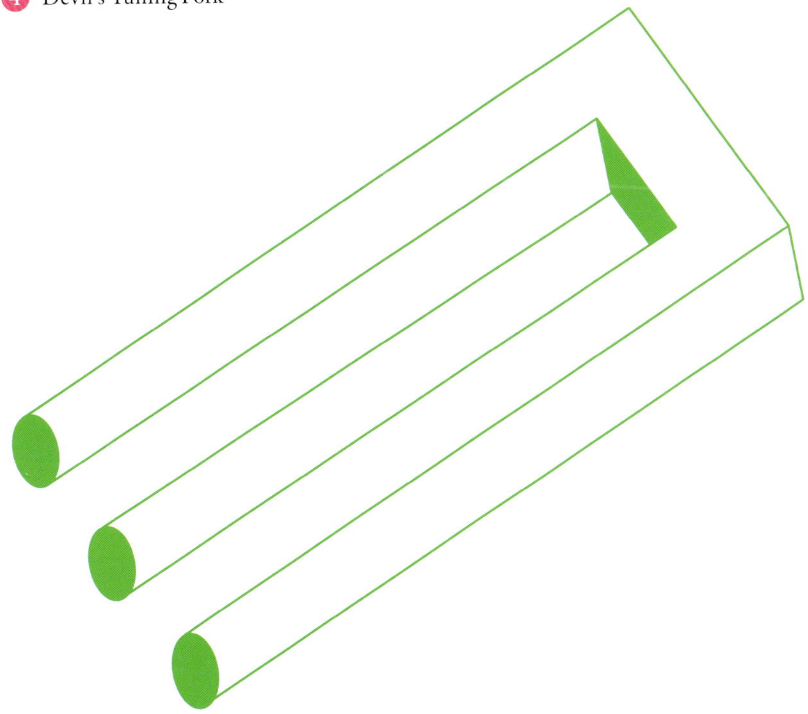

The Devil's Tuning Fork, also known as the impossible trident, appears to have three cylindrical prongs at one end which then mysteriously transform into two rectangular prongs at the other end.

[1]Source from Wikipedia

Project Impossible in Green and Orange was inspired by Oscar Reutersvärd's *Impossible Tribar*(Penrose Triangle).
While designing this project, the tribars, one is divided into cubes, were placed in pseudo-3D space and drawn with distorted, high-contrast lines of two colors—green and black or orange and black.

If you observe carefully, you can see that the colors of the tribars are the opposite of the colors of the background. While the lines of the background are black, the color of the tribar will be green or orange, making it contrast with the background. Finally, these "impossible" tribars seem to float in front of the background.

IMPOSSIBLE IN GREEN AND ORANGE

Design: Robert Voight

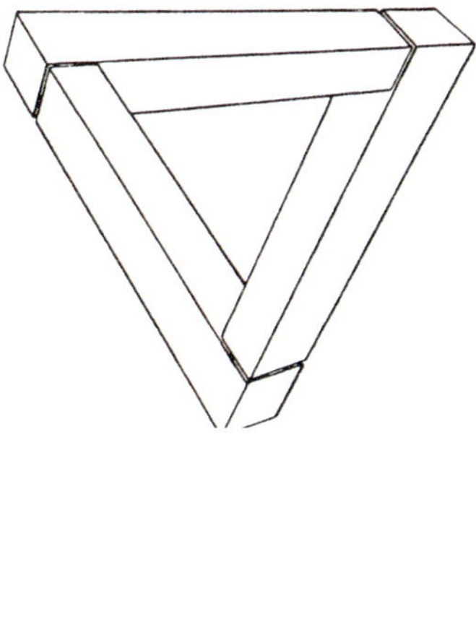

PROJECT 02064

Design: Robert Voight

This is an advertising poster for a company specializing in printing and typography. The full-color, pseudo-3-D pattern on the poster seems to be ordered, but it is distorted.

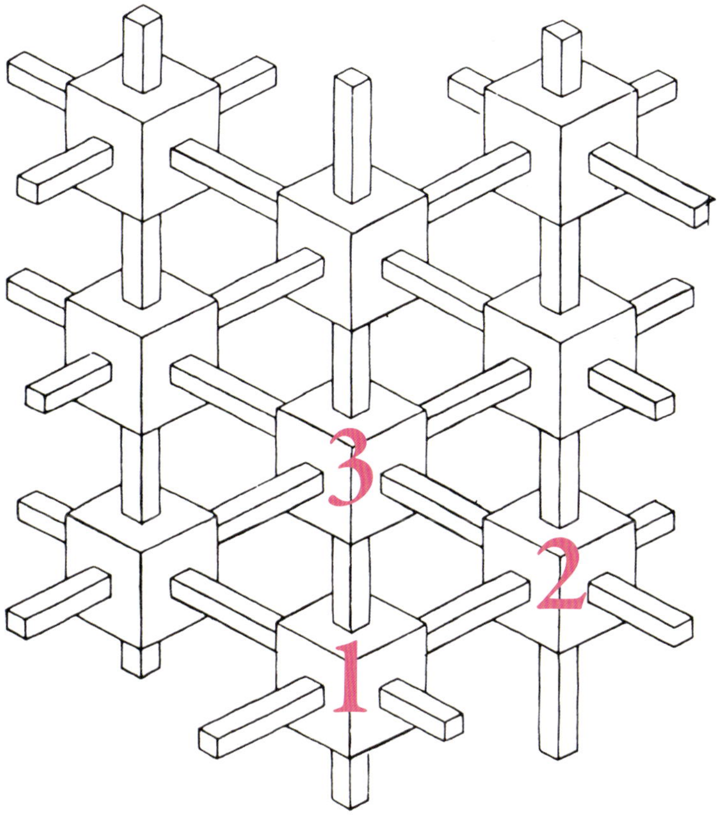

Taking the Grids 1, 2, and 3 as examples, Grids 1 and 2 are arranged side by side. Grid 2 is on the right side of Grid 1. Grids 2 and 3 are also arranged side by side. Grid 3 is behind Grid 2. However, while looking at Grids 1 and 3, we can see that Grid 3 is above Grid 1, which is impossible in real life. Here, the designer uses sticks to connect these grids together and creates the distorted space.

1

BLIND explores paradoxical situations in society today through the posters of paradoxical images and optical illusions, in hopes of inspiring the audience to be more careful with the information they receive, to reflect, and to think critically before drawing conclusions.

BLIND

Design: Lowei Chang, Steve Huang

2

Blind Following[1]

Viral trends are a major social phenomenon in Taiwan. A popular news story, a short video from the Internet, or an article all have the potential to go viral. However, many of people have become addicted to the sharing and reposting of information without checking for legitimacy, causing them to slowly start to accept unreliable information.

Rumors spread from person to person like viruses. The problem is further amplified by the credibility of media outlets that publish these stories, creating a false sense of validity and making people fall into a continuous loop as in the Penrose Stairs.

People should escape this infinite loop and avoid blindly following trends and jumping onto popular bandwagons by remaining rational, and thinking critically about things before acting.

Solar Energy[2]

This pattern is based on the Penrose Triangle, which is the impossible tribar. It aims to arouse people's reflection on solar energy: are clean energies as clean as we think they are?

In regions of abundant sunshine, solar energy can be harnessed to create a seemingly endless supply of energy, without creating greenhouse gas by-products which lead to global warming. Unfortunately, as the production of solar energy grows larger in scale, it also causes side effects which are destructive to ecosystems and environments.

For instance, light reflected by the mirrors in solar energy production will raise the temperature in surrounding areas, doing harm to the creatures in the sky or on the ground. Solar energy is a double-edged sword. It reveals that the human search for clean energy inevitably leads to undesirable side effects, just like the Penrose Triangle, it is both self-contradictory and self-circulating.

THINK
AGAIN ?
/
DON'T
JUDGE
TOO
QUICKLY !
BLIND
Don't judge too quickly, it May Not be what you think!
Department of Visual Design, NKNU
Graduation Project ' BLIND ' AGU 2015 -
By Lowei Chang / Steve Huang

THINK
AGAIN ?
/
DON'T
JUDGE
TOO
QUICKLY !
BLIND
Department of Visual Design, NKNU
By Lowei Chang / Steve Huang

4

Equality[3]

Inspired by Café Wall Illusion, this poster makes people pay attention to the true equality.

People are born into different circumstances; therefore, what benefits one person may have the opposite effect on another. Seeking equality through homogenization often sacrifices individuality, and ironically creates inequality. In the search of equality, people must pay more attention in creating the true equality, rather than a superficial appearance, just like the Café Wall Illusion which does not seem parallel apparently, but the horizontal lines are parallel to each other.

Personal Relationships[4]

Thanks to the rapid development of technology, friends and families are now able to get in touch with each other easily, at any time, and over long distances. As people begin to recognize that contact is just a touch of a fingertip away, however, they've become less inclined to make the effort to meet face to face.

As a result, although people enjoy the convenience provided by technology, they do so at a price of separation. While technology can connect people in different spaces, it can also distance people in the same space. A cold screen is like the illusion of staircase in which people can't tell up and down, is the distance between people closer or further?

IMAGINE THE POSSIBILITIES

Design: Magpie Studio

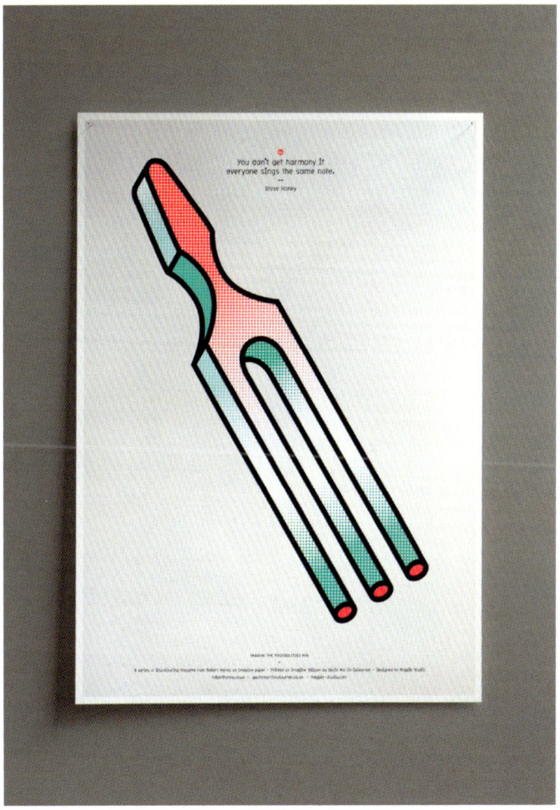

This series of limited edition prints are designed for an international paper manufacturer—the Robert Horne Group. The concept is underpinned by creative thinking and visual games. Borrowed from Escher's impossible drawings, each illusion is drafted by hand on an isometric grid, aiming to inspire imagination and creative thinking.

While designing the letter sequence D, J, and O,the designer created the downward depression or deep visual effect by overlapping circles or polygons of different sizes.

While designing the letters F and K, shadow was used to create the different levels.

While designing *36 Days of Type III*, the designer applied principles of visual illusion to the differing shapes of letters or numbers.

36 DAYS OF TYPE III

Design: Riccardo Sabatini

Considering the shapes of the letter H and numbers 3 and 36, the designer used lines to connect the different sides of the cuboids, bringing the illusion that these sides are facing in the same dimension.

Finally, referring to the impossible tribar, the designer distorted the numbers 4 and 7 to the shapes that are unavailable physically.

This optical illusion design was inspired by Oscar Reutersvärd's 3-D drawings, which appear structurally feasible at first glance but are in fact impossible to physically construct.

The designer applied this formula to create the letter shapes. She duplicated a letter stroke and placed the copy counter-intuitively, off from the original letter, and created paths between the letter points.

OPTICAL ILLUSION TYPE DESIGN

Design: Eunsol Lee

HAPPY,
NEW
YEAR

A
B
C
H
I
J
O
P
Q
V
W
X

This alphabet design consists of various vibrant visual elements. In addition, points, lines, and planes filled with various colors are used to attract attention.

TRIBUTE TO THE MASTERS OF DECEPTION

Design: Jibin Shaji

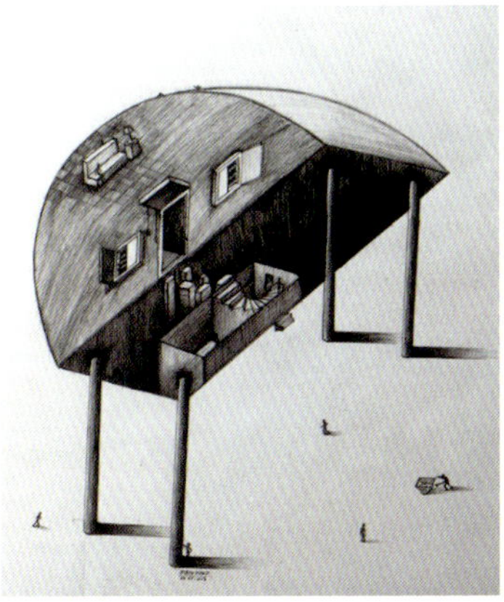

Usually we see things from a point of view. What we see, however, may be different from the real world.
Inspired by the Penrose Triangle and the Op-art movement, artist Jibin Shaji incorporated into his artwork the thought that "There are two sides to everything."

Tribute to The Masters of Deception: an exploration of illusion using different perspective angles and foreground-background confusion. When viewing the corner, one can see what looks like a corner of a ceiling and at the same time looks like the edge of a terrace.

The inspiration for this illusion artwork was the *Penrose Stairs*, an optical illusion of a staircase with no ending and no beginning. The participant appears to be ascending or descending the stairs, depending on where he or she stands in relation to the work of art.
Painted via a water-based tempera medium, this work was created using anamorphic projection principles requiring the viewer to use a camera or occupy a specific vantage point to see the correct version of the image. The image appears distorted and unrecognizable when seen from most angles. When one views it from the proper viewing location with a camera, however, the optical illusion reveals itself wonderfully.

TECHRITI' 14 FESTIVAL – 3-D PENROSE STAIRCASE

Design: Tracy Lee Stum

Penrose Stairs

INTERNET EXPLORER

Design: Ellaisweird

This is a poster design based on the theme of "Internet" for a children's magazine.

▲ Shift in upside-down perception

The Internet is like an adventure land where people can explore and visit anywhere without physically being there. It is filled with mysteries, surprises, knowledge, and secrets: all waiting to be found. To show its mystery, the designer hid a few funny visual illusions in the poster, such as patterns that are 2-D but look like 3-D, by using combinations of lines and colors, and shifting in upside-down perceptions, and motion illusions that appear as if they are moving due to the luminance grating.

▲ 2-D patterns which look like 3-D

▲ Motion illusion

EDGE PERCEPTION

Sensory perception of edges can be evoked by changing the arrangement of lines or graphics, connecting the various components of the graphics to form a complete image. Then the observer will see a non-existent, illusory contour.

1 Change the curvature of lines.

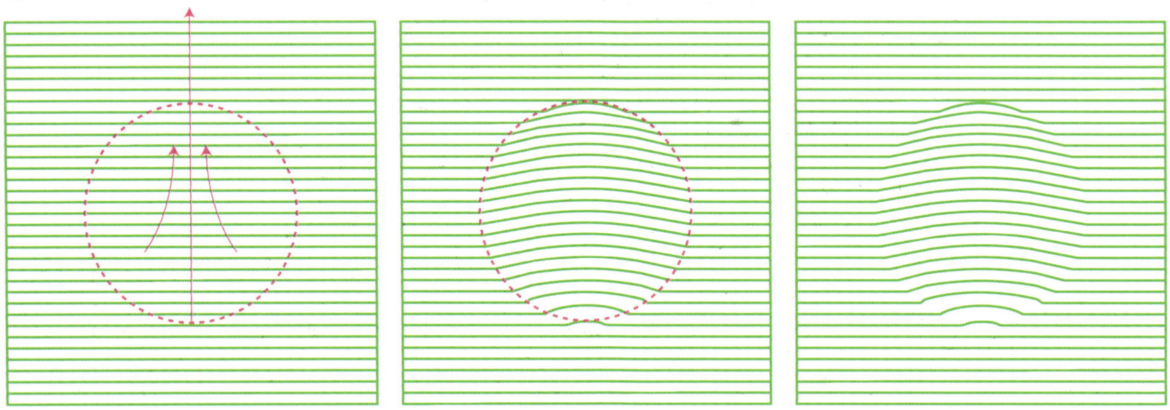

2 Change the direction of lines.

DO IT YOURSELF!

Let's try to make this hand three-dimensional!

Tips:

DOLCE

Design: La Come Di

The designs are part of the clothing line "Dolce" by La Come Di. Dolce series takes inspiration from Mediterranean lifestyle and retells these stories using a minimalist aesthetic.

The main idea of the series is to capture that lifestyle from real life and embed it within the stripes to create an optical art that brings those experiences to life. The end result creates an illusion onto what seems like familiar stripes, but with a little story told between its lines.

These notebooks were designed to celebrate the 10th anniversary of QKunst. For the cover, the designer created a typographic system where a grid of lines is bent and broken to form the shape of the letters within the grid.

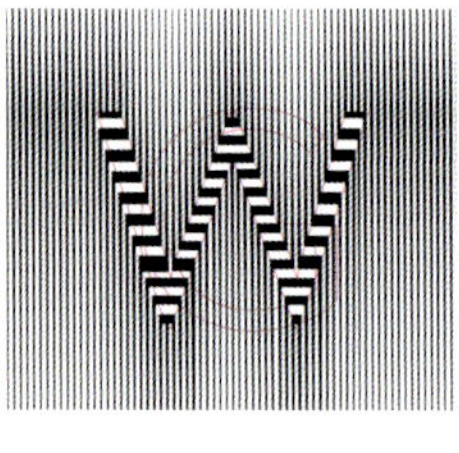

10 YEARS QKUNST

Design: Hansje van Halem Studio

A Birthday Poster ▲

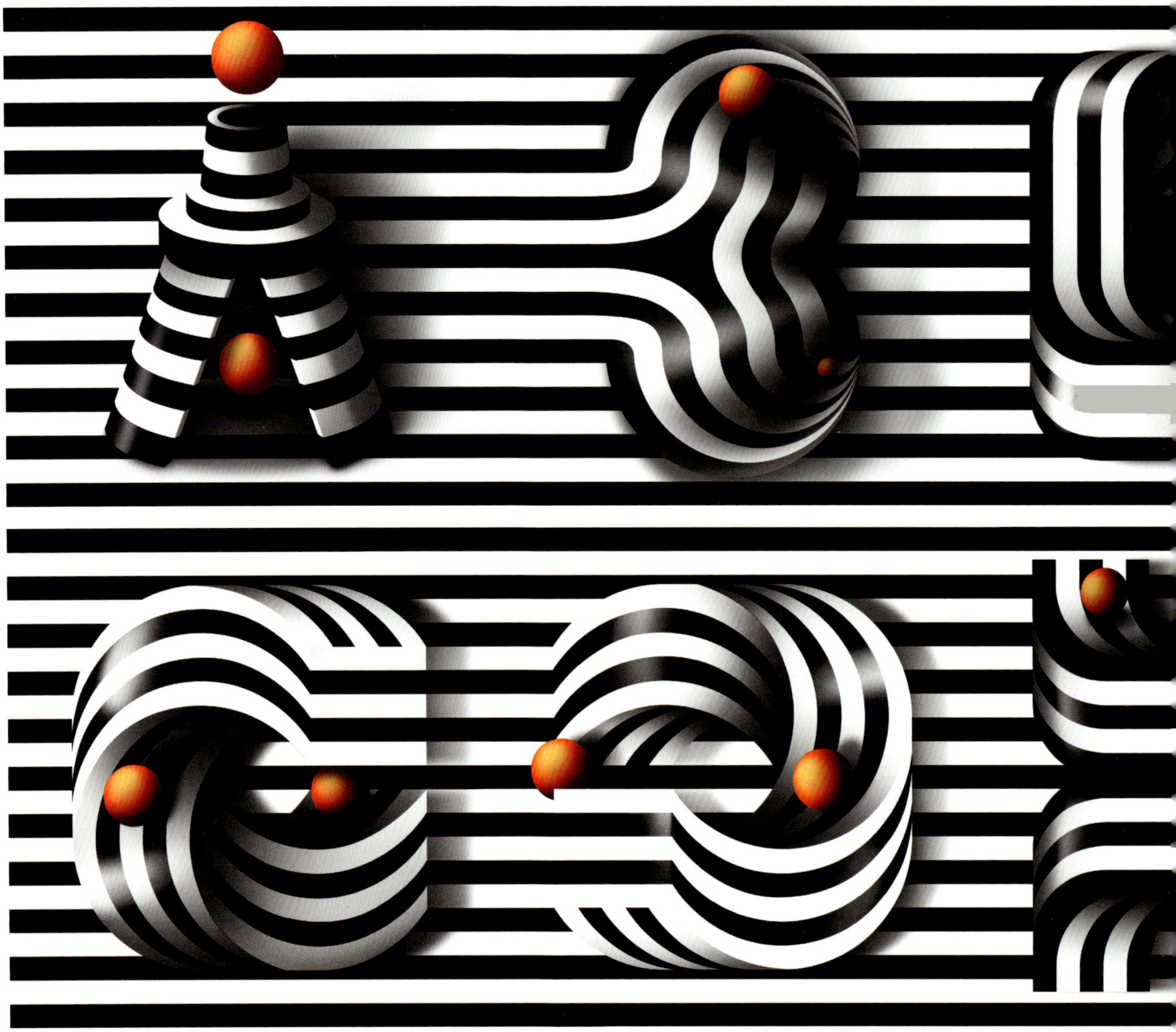

This alphabet is based on Op Art. The foreground (all the letters) and the background of patterns both consist of black and white stripes.

Each letter is made to seem like a moving artistic game. Black and white stripes in the background are misplaced and distorted to various directions to create the shapes of different letters. Shadows in the background strengthen the three-dimensional effect.
The designer also used orange balls to make colors contrast, coupled with the twisted letters, making the balls look as if they are flowing onto the letters.

OP-ART ALPHABET

Design:DAQ

1

These illustrations with different themes and marked styles are designed for three mobile phone cases, they are Faces, Geometric, and Op art.

VIRGIN MOBILE UK

Design:DAQ

2

3

Faces[1]

In this illustration, the designer distorted the words 4G WITH above the people's faces in the background, creating a visual deception in which the viewer feels as if the words are waving in the air.

Geometric[2]

This design consists of floating geometric modules. These modules are stretched along the words 4G WITH in the middle, enhancing the floating effect in space. The designer used only a few simple colors, such as green, yellow, and orange, to render the geometric modules. He then highlighted the words 4G WITH in white.

Op Art[3]

The designer used some repeating lines to create this abstract composition. He cast a shadow under the distortion of these lines so that the distorted part would seem to protrude forward.

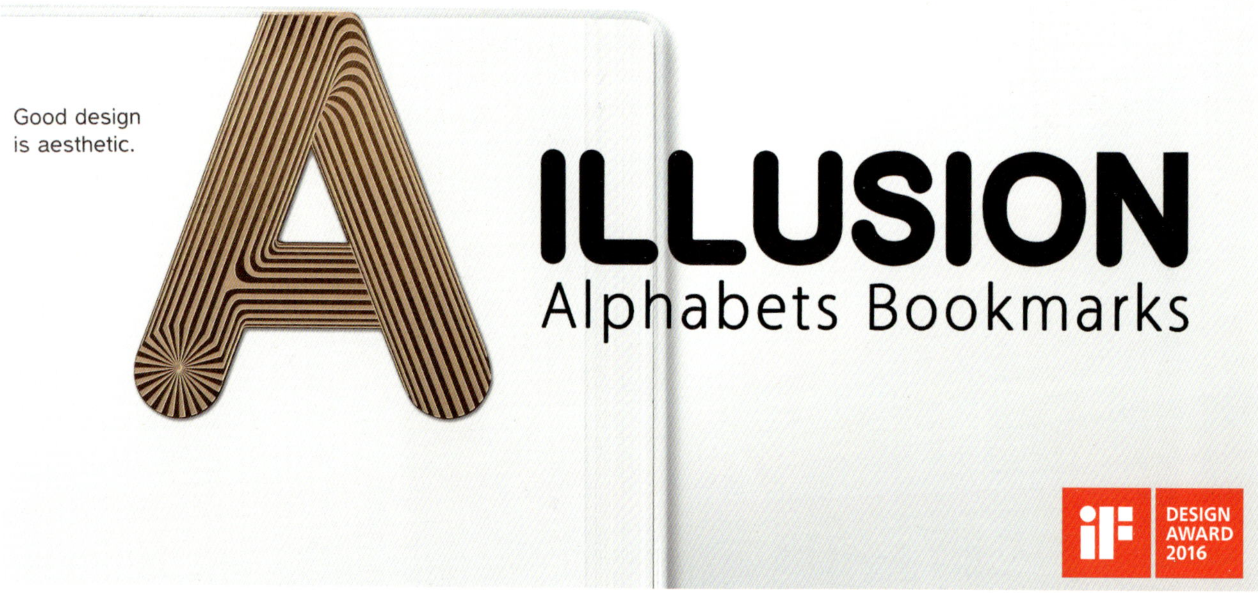

This series of alphabet bookmarks combines metal etching patterns and a complex, variable font design. Based on a circular front, the strokes of each bookmark consist of stripes. At the turning point, the deformation of the stripes of the circular tube is realized by the change of arc and overlap, creating a wonderful depth effect in space.

ILLUSION ALPHABET BOOKMARKS

Design: PHAIdesign

A closer look reveals that these "striped circular tubes" provide a stunning three-dimensional effect. The realistic deformation makes this three-dimensional effect and the visual illusion difficult to distinguish, creating endless fun and steric strain in the work. The metal texture of the bookmarks even strengthens this illusion.

HAPPY

BON
VOYAGE
BUDAPEST
PRAHA

CEST LAVIE
SALON DE

MARRY
ME

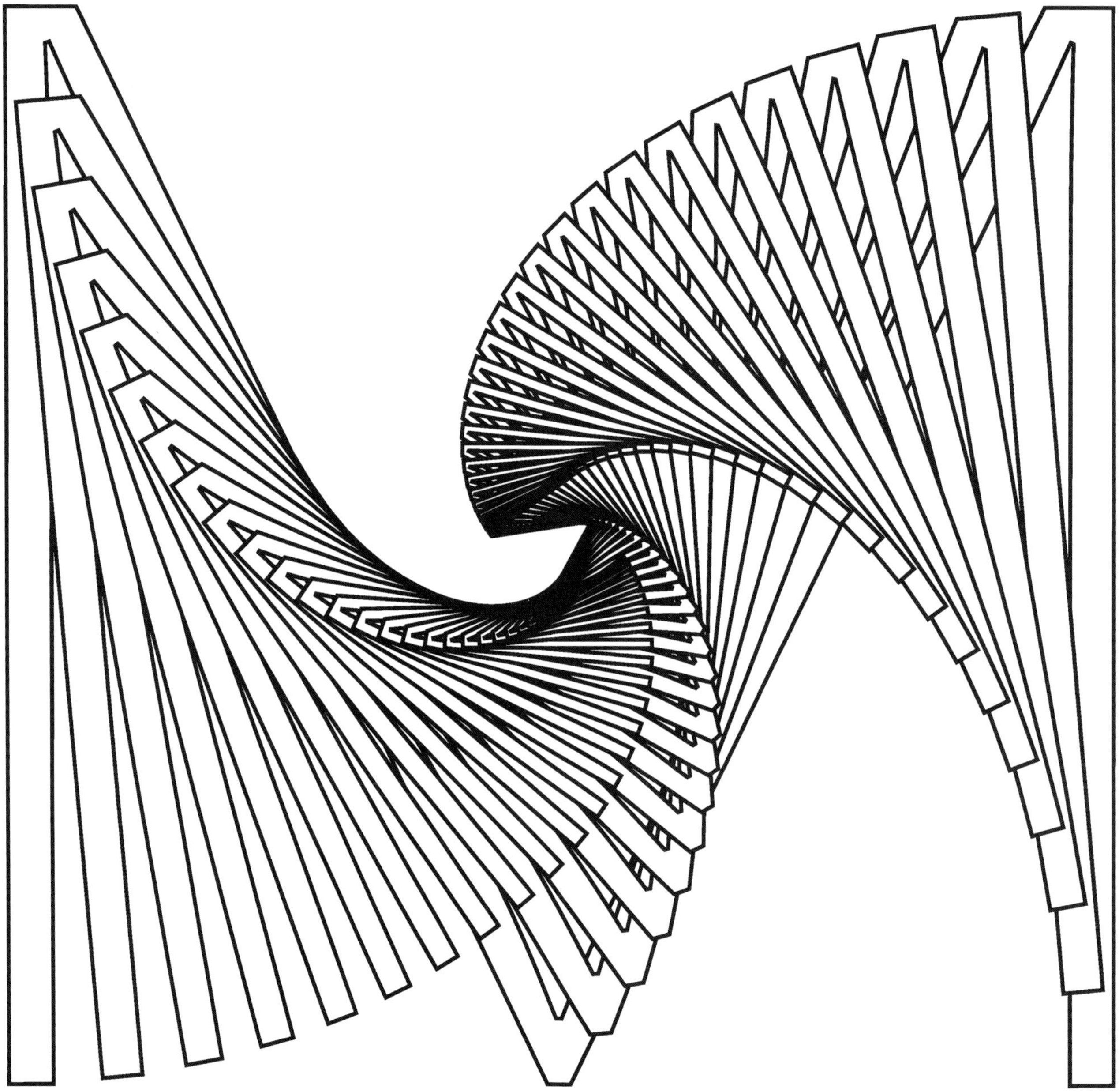

This design project of 26 English letters creates illusions of movement and depth within the flat and static sheet of paper. Lines that construct the contours of letters rotate to the middle point, expressing the visual ideas of distortion and dimension.

DYNAMISM OF TYPOGRAPHIC FORM

Design:Silvia Baz

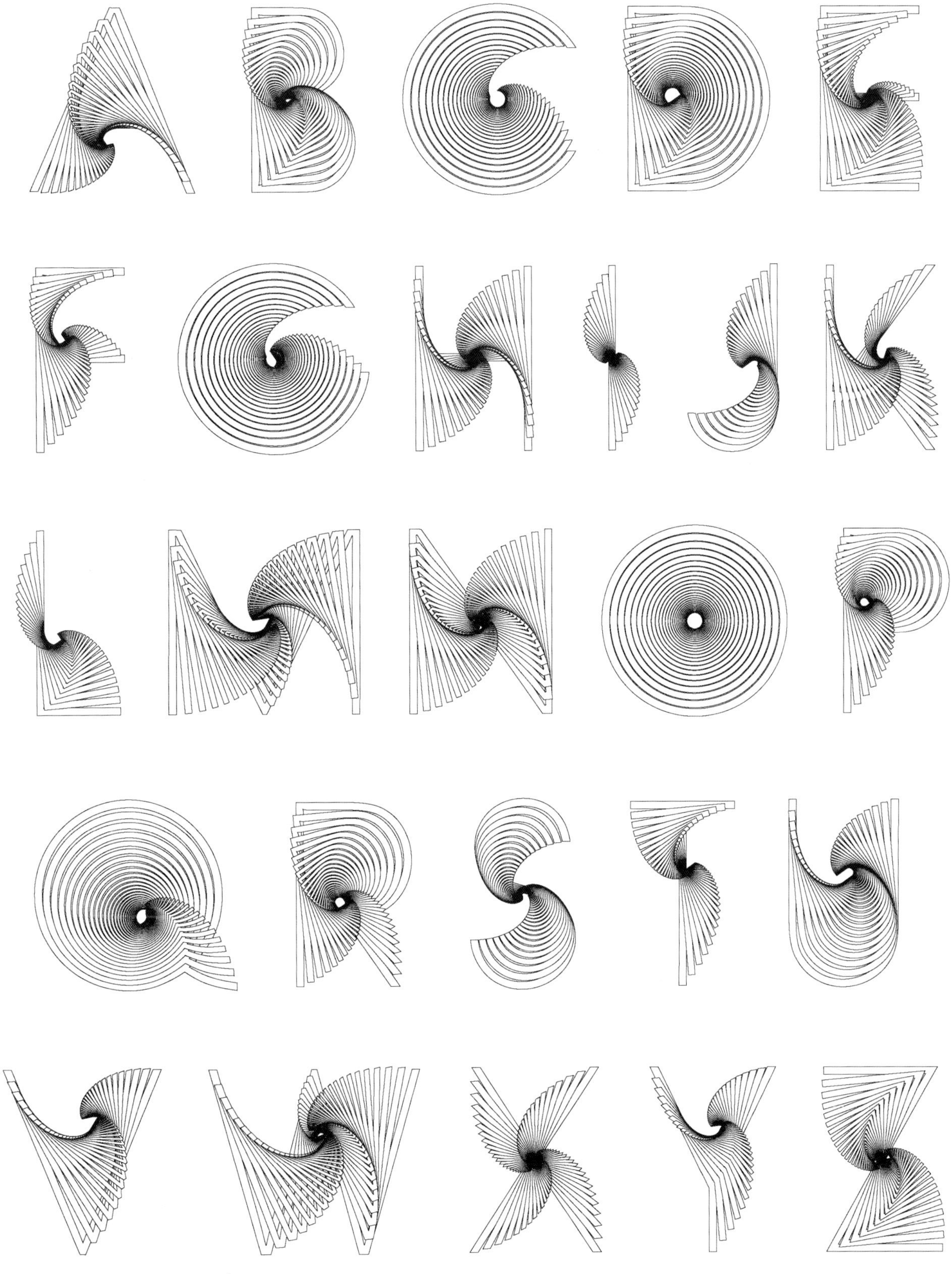

OPTILABS/WAVES

Design: Riccardo Sabatini

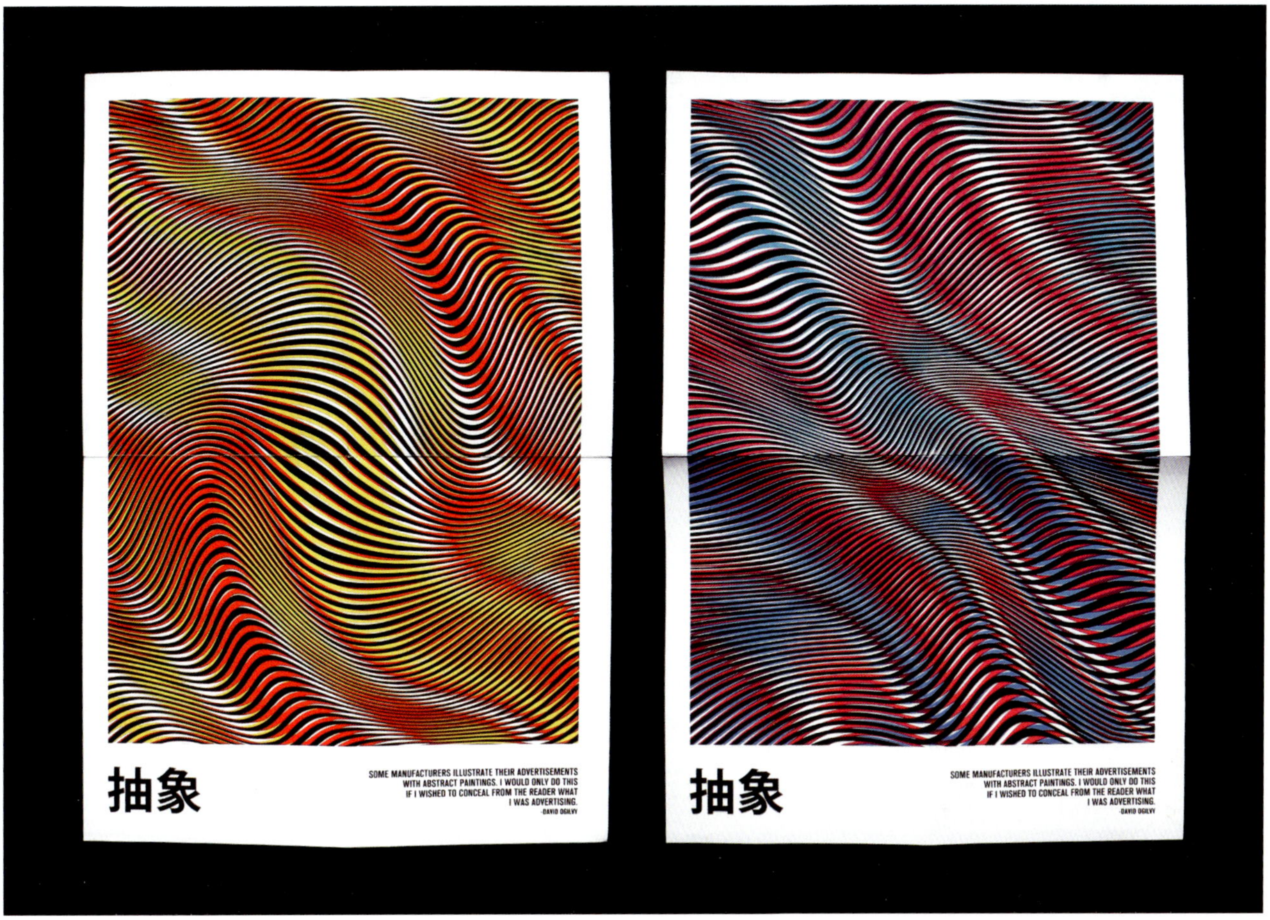

Optilabs/Waves is a series of abstract patterns like optical illusions and Moiré patterns.[1] Sinusoidal lines are combined and overlaid to create the rolling-wave pattern.

[1]Moiré pattern, or moiré fringes, are the large-scale interference patterns that can be produced when an opaque ruled pattern with transparent gaps is overlaid on another similar pattern.

UZURI—CLASSIC AND SEASONAL MAKEUP COLLECTIONS

Design:Chloe Galea Client: Uzuri

Uzuri is a premium makeup brand using 100% natural organic ingredients. Inspired by optical illusionary art, a series of monotone patterns were produced, highlighting the concept that makeup itself can be used to create optical illusions. These patterns created a striking and original packaging solution, which was bold enough to stand out in the competitive beauty market.

Small details were also considered. For example, contrasting patterns were applied to the insides of the packaging and stickers were pasted to show the makeup colors.

UZURI
UZURI

UZURI
Foundation
natural / illuminating
/ medium coverage
summer sun
UZURI
UZURI
LUCY ROSE

ILLUSION is one of the oldest movie houses in Russia. Several times a year this movie house would focus on specific themes (i.e., French/Hungarian/Czech/Norwegian movie festivals, Arthouse movies of the 80s/90s), which were the starting points and the inspirations for these creations.

The designer created light patterns by setting the color palette and composition, and the after-images of certain colors would then appear on lines, finally integrated within the design.

ILLUSION GRAPHICS

Design:Daria Krisel

БУМ—
новой волны
французского
кинематографа
13.09
14.09
15.09
НОВОЕ КИНО
ФРАНЦИИ
10.09
11.09
12.09
БУМ
новой волны
французского

РЕТРО—
СПЕКТИВА
КИНО ВЕНГРИИ
ЛУЧШИЕ ФИЛЬМЫ
ЗА ПОСЛЕДНИЕ 20 ЛЕТ
2012
09.04
16.04—
НОВОЕ КИНО
ВЕНГРИИ
17.04
24.04
2012
НОВОЕ ПОКОЛЕНИЕ
ВЕНГЕРСКИХ РЕЖИССЕРОВ
НОВОЕ
КИНО ВЕНГРИИ

13.12
ГОСТИ
Писатель
и режиссер
Томас Каппелен Маллинг;
Писатель Даг
Сульстад;
Режиссер
и сценарист
НОРВЕЖСКОГО КИНО
ДНИ НОРВЕЖСКОГО
НОРВЕЖСКОГО КИНО
20.12

КИНО
ИСПАНИИ
7.06
АМАДОР
13.06
9.06
НОВОЕ
ПОКОЛЕНИЕ
ИСПАНСКИХ
РЕЖИССЕРОВ

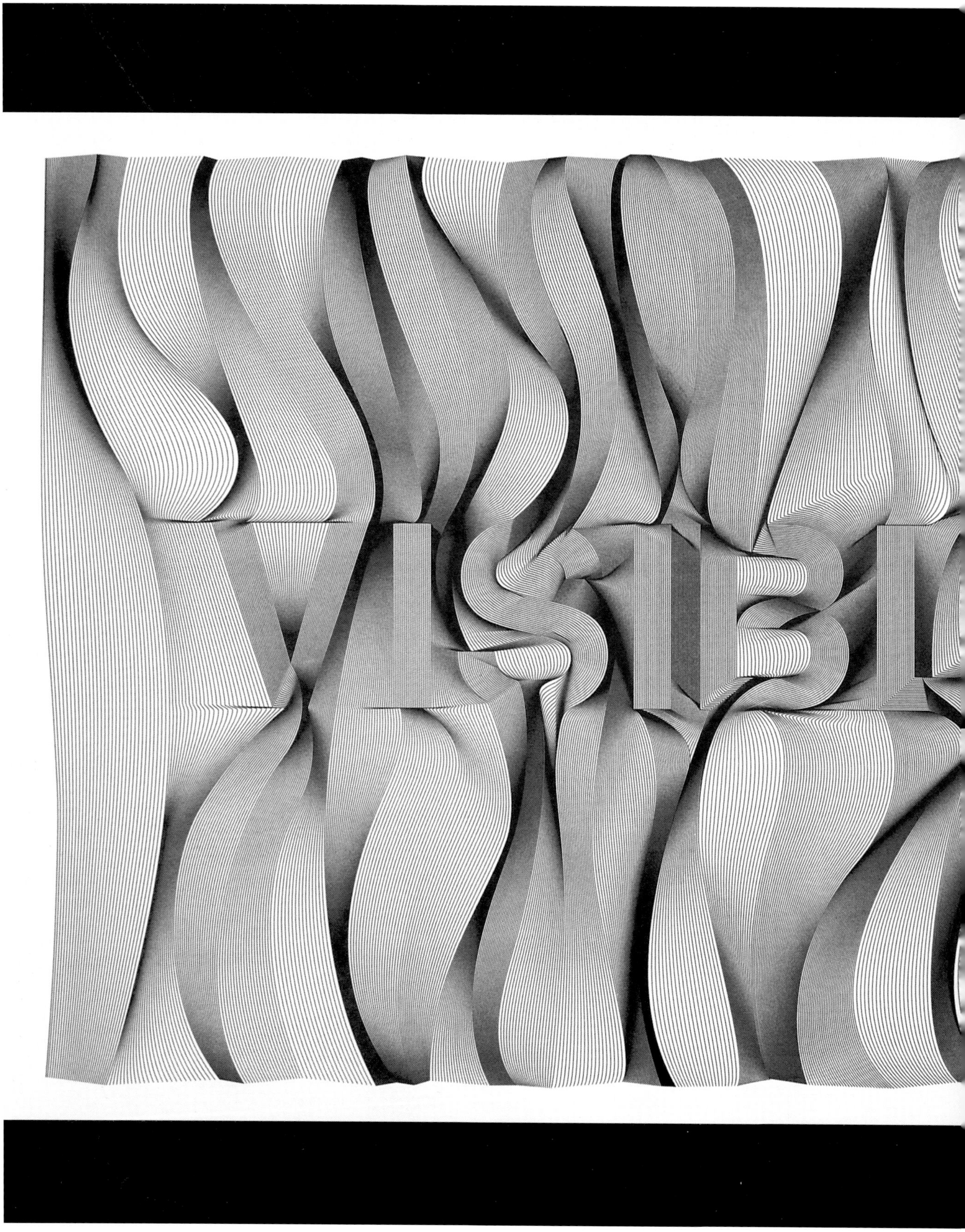

**RIDICULOUS TYPOGRAPHY RULES—
ILLUSTRATED TYPOGRAPHY**

Design: Leon Dijkstra

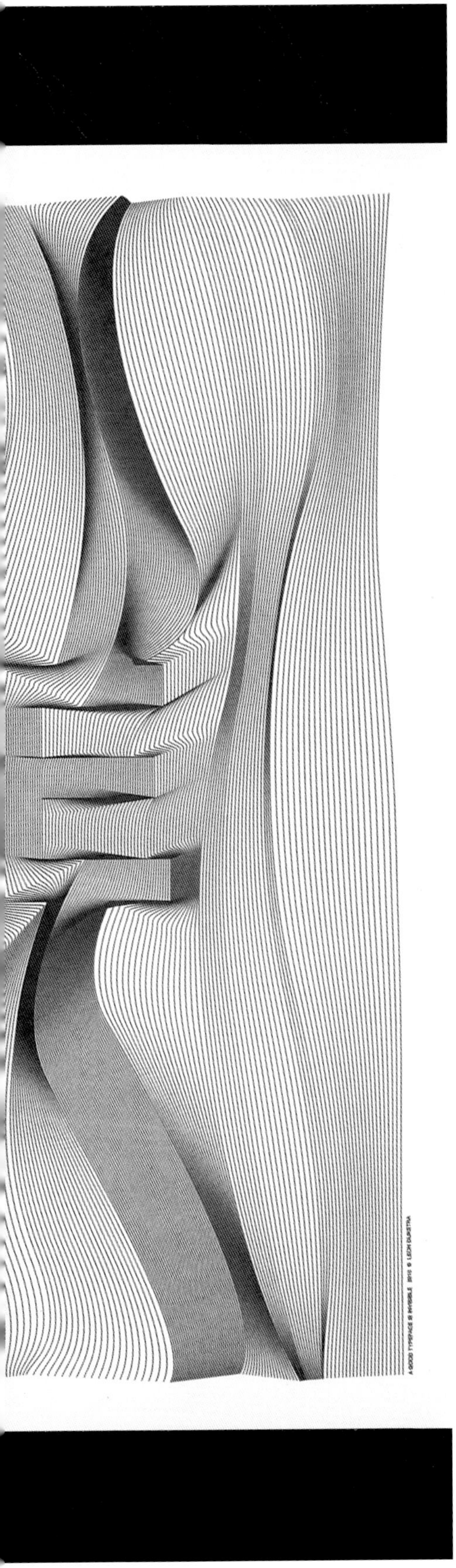

When seeing text as typographical image, designer Leon Dijkstra starts to think, "Why not change the image into text?" To make this come true, the most critical problem he needed to solve was the interaction of visibility and legibility between image and text.

The designer directly distorted the lines in the image into the shapes of different letters, which made the letters seem to be flowing. By combining publication design and visual identity, he visualized the message behind the brand.

With the advent of new digital technologies, Peter Kogler began to extend painting into three-dimensional space. He tried to change people's views of space by using painting at the frontiers of abstraction and blurring the architecture. In his artistic projects, the audience became the protagonist.

To make the floating walls, Peter first digitalized the images which are computer generated, then magnified and organized them on the surface of the wallpaper.
The simple black-and-white grid provided maximum contrast, which offers a strong visual presence.

The structure of the image is comprehensive and surrounds the beholder. In a sense, people are standing in the picture, and the work can be experienced physically, in which their bodies are caught in a labyrinthine relationship between a physical place and a virtual space.

In the warped room, the infinite lines appear as a representation of man lost, losing himself as he searches for self-knowledge.

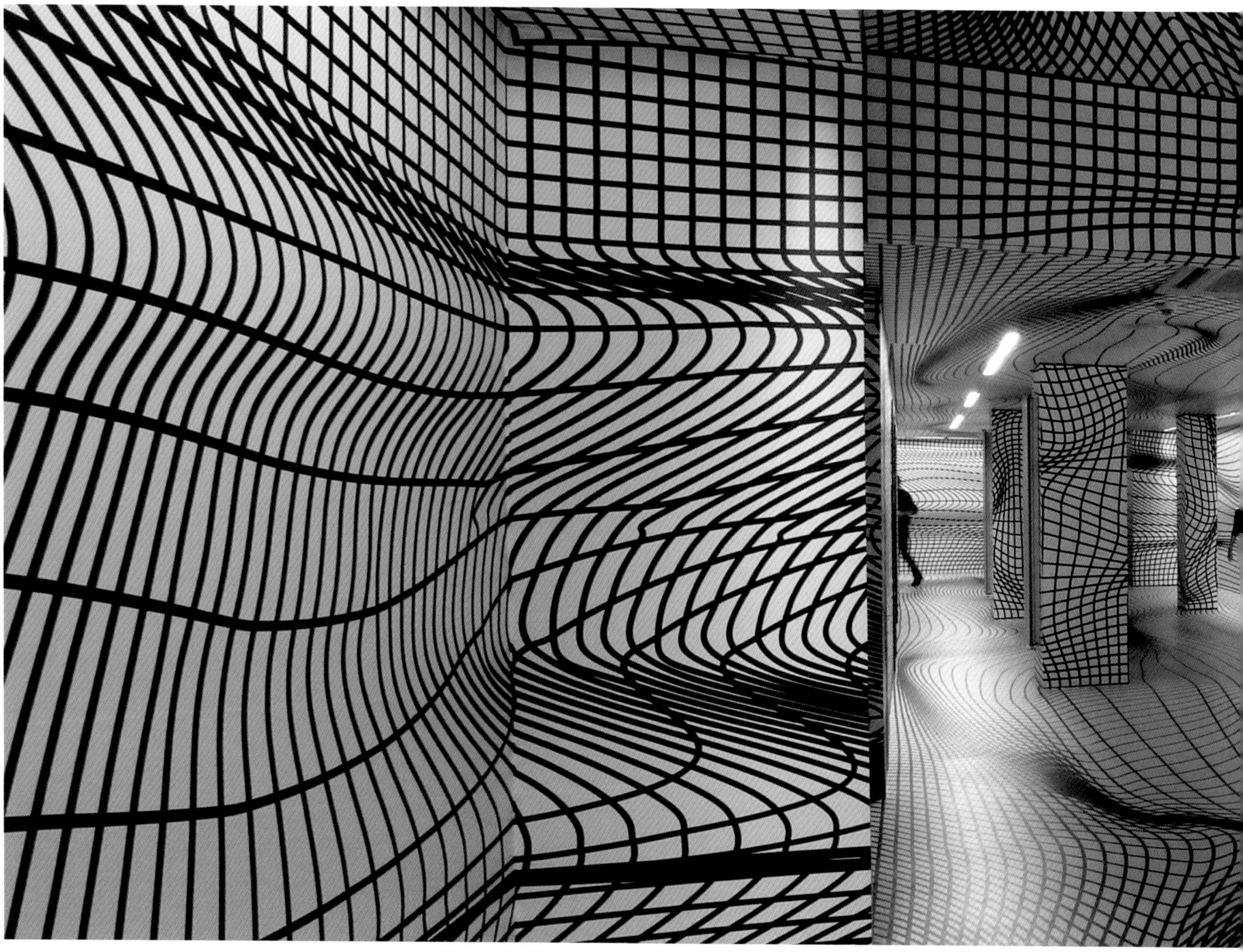

VISUALLY WARPED ROOMS

Design:Peter Kogler

Diffusion is a dance studio not only for ordinary people, but also for deaf and blind people.

DANCE STUDIO "DIFFUSION"

Design:Daria Yakushina

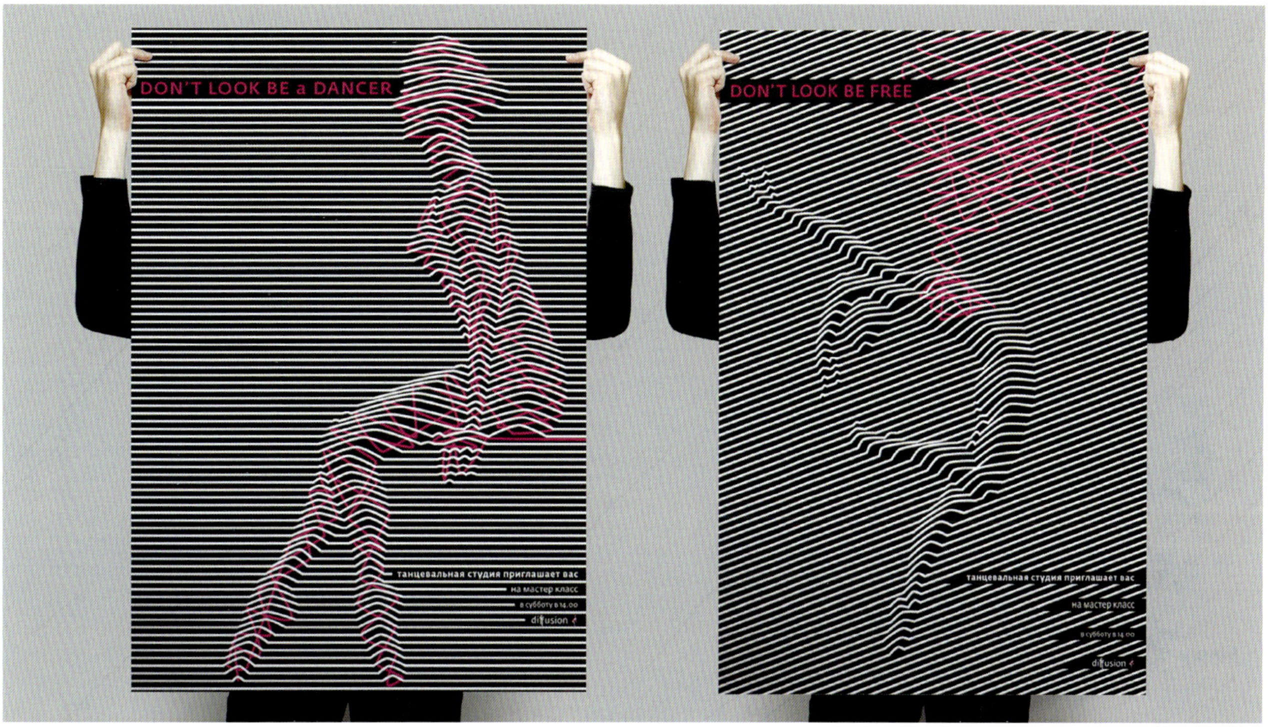

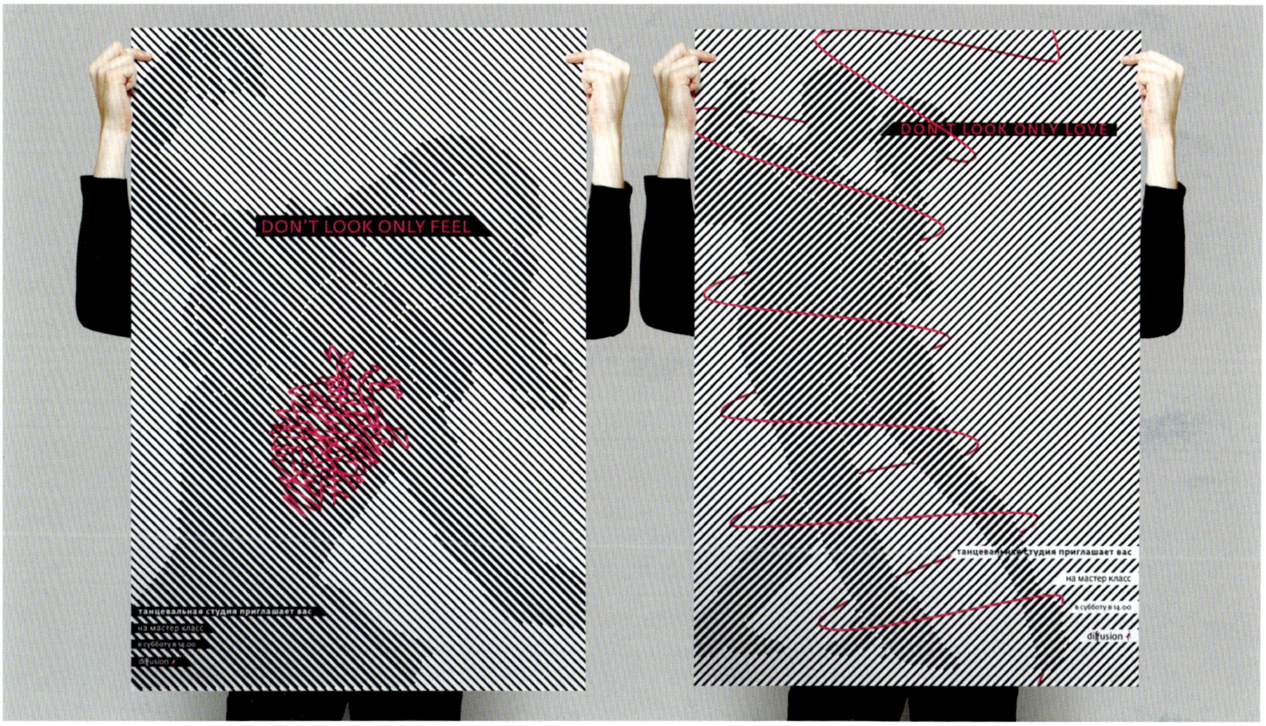

The designer used bold black lines to create a three-dimensional human shape, or simply used two different-colored lines to outline the shape of a dancing person.

diffusion

These intersecting lines erase the boundaries between people and show the deep intimacy between them, which is also the vision of the dance studio.

SPIRAL ILLUSION

A sequence of tilted elements caused by overlapping regular concentric circles makes the eyes feel the distortion of illusion and envision a spiral.

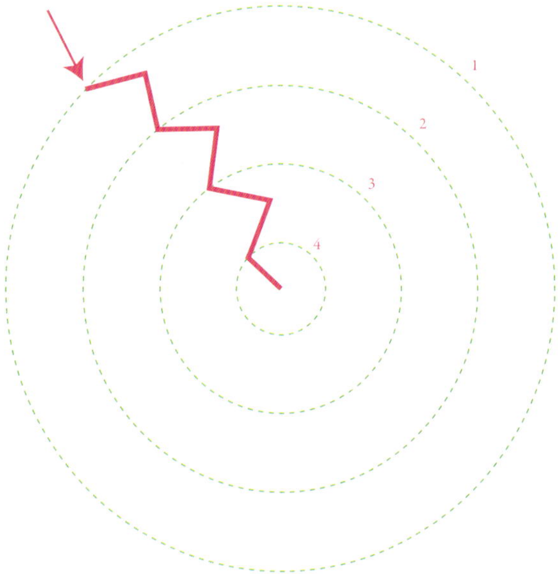

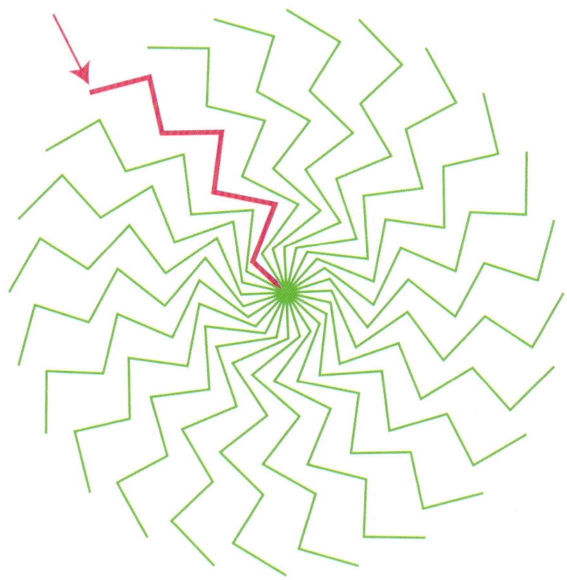

DO IT YOURSELF!

1. Fill the color block in a specific order.

2. Place the object in the center of the circle.

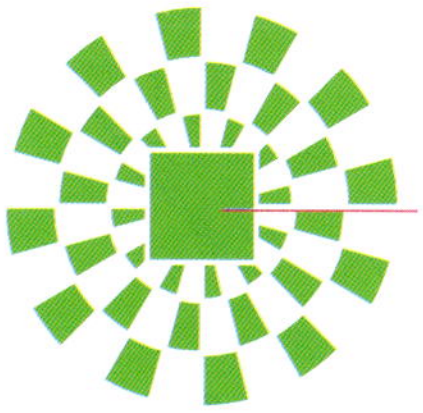

3. Now, take a photo perpendicular to the center of the circle.

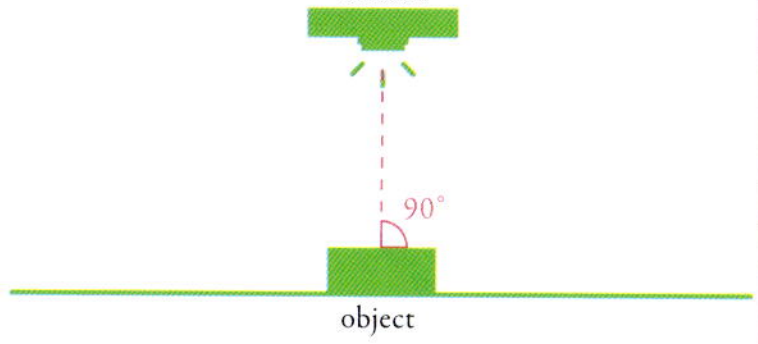

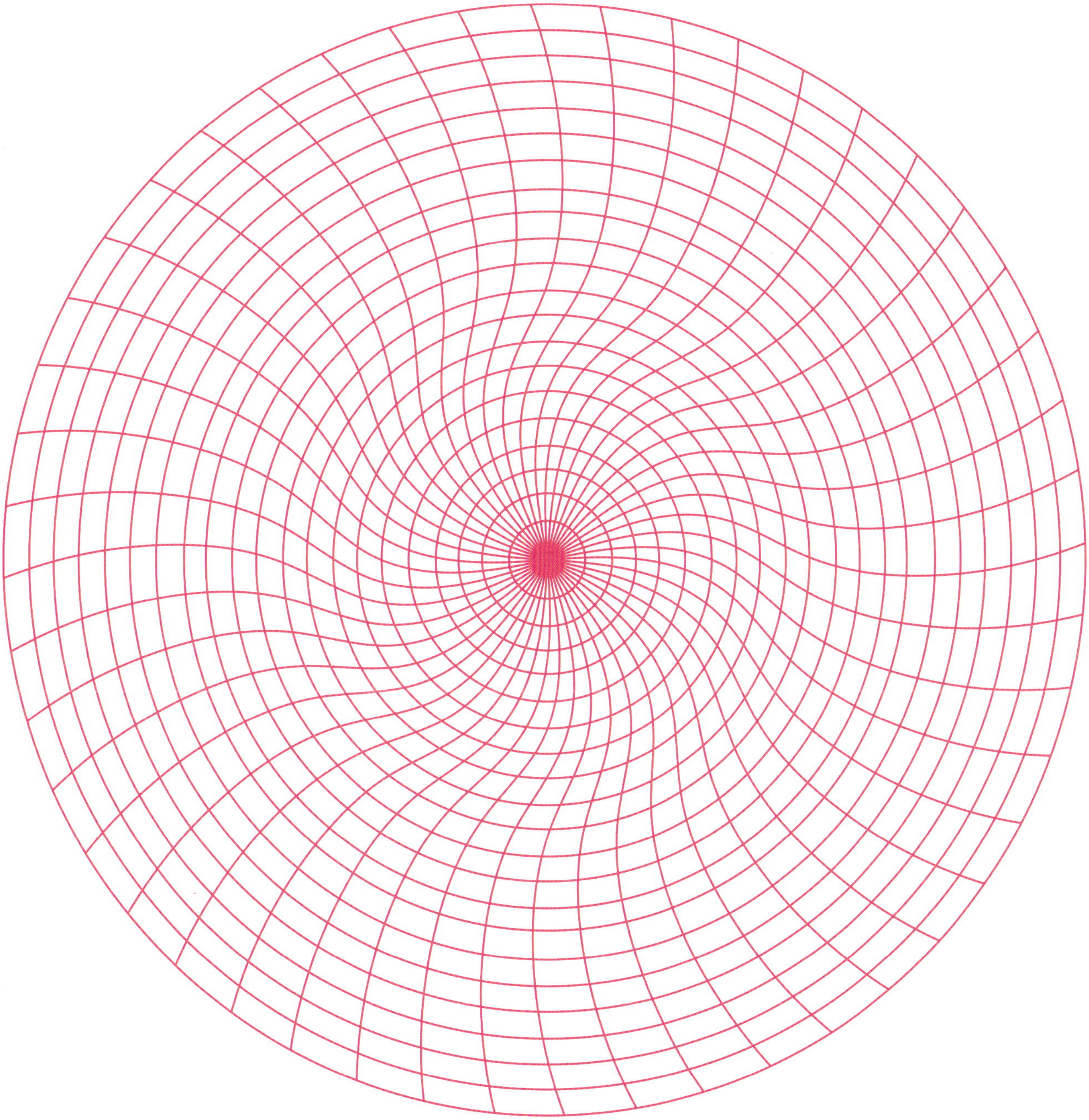

When creating this campaign, the first thing the designer focused on was the wide product range of the brand. To attract the public's attention, the designer created a striking and eye-catching design.

With bright colors that match the color of the product itself, he used a rotating pattern as the background, and then placed the product in the middle of the image, making it the focal point.

BOYNER EVDE ADVERTISING

Design:Emrah Eşki

boyner
evde
When you can't take your eyes off it, just take it. Let's bring some style to your home with Boyner Evde. boynerevde.com.tr

T-BOX
Genç, enerjik, eğlenceli, özgün ve maceraperest
boyner
evde
When you can't take your eyes off it, just take it.

When you can't take your eyes off it, just take it. Let's bring

When you can't take your eyes off it, just take it. Let's brin

boyner
evde

When you can't take your eyes off it, just take it. Let's brin

Opus Motus are made of colored marbles. The geometric layouts of the disks can be seen when the pieces are still.

However, once the disks are rotating at a certain speed, the colors merge together, forming other unprecedented shades and creating circular patterns. This optical effect produced by movement is based on persistence of vision.

Colors on the rotating wheels mix together if the motion is too fast to register the details. A colored dot then appears as a circle, and one line can make the whole surface appear as one uniform hue. The visual explosion of colors and shapes reveals to every onlooker unique and surprising optical effects.

OPUS MOTUS

Design:Raffaello Galiotto   Company:Lithos Design

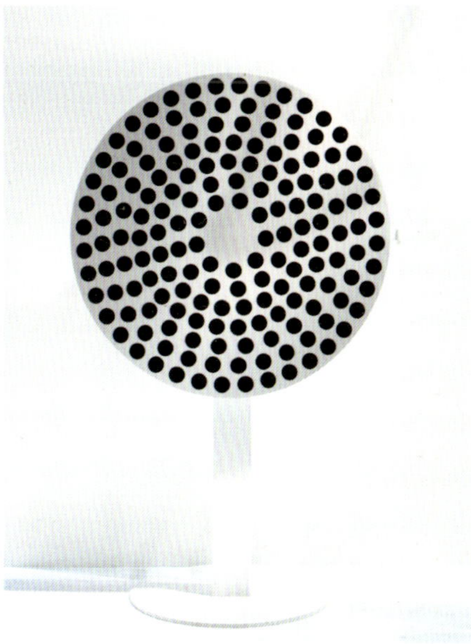

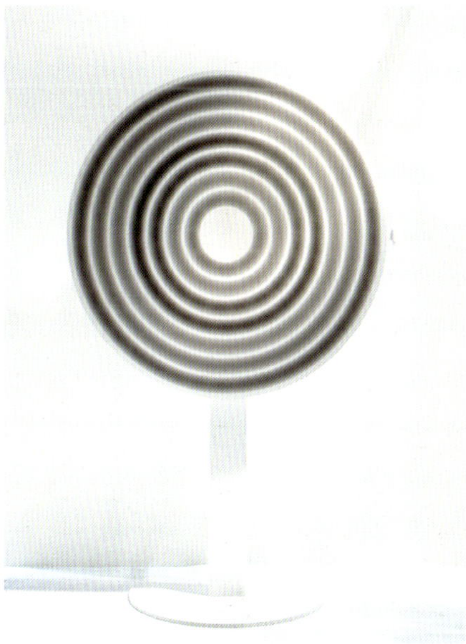

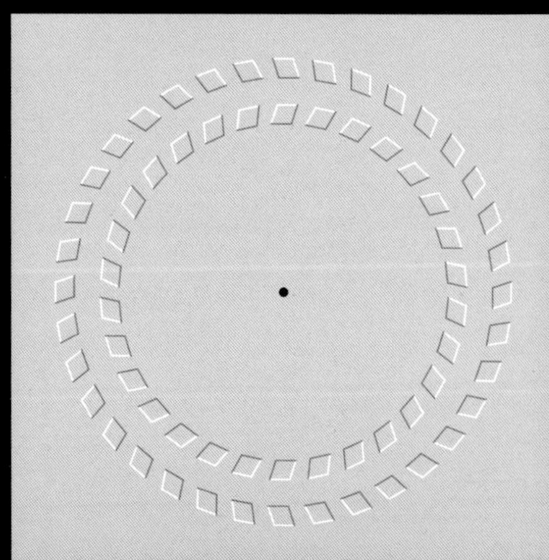

This is the cover for GUILT.: a vinyl record made via illusion techniques. Focusing on the text in the center of the cover and moving the head backwards and forwards, the pointing-hand image on the cover creates a movement illusion.

DARIUS VAIKAS—GUILT. VINYL RECORD

Design:Denis Kuchta Studio

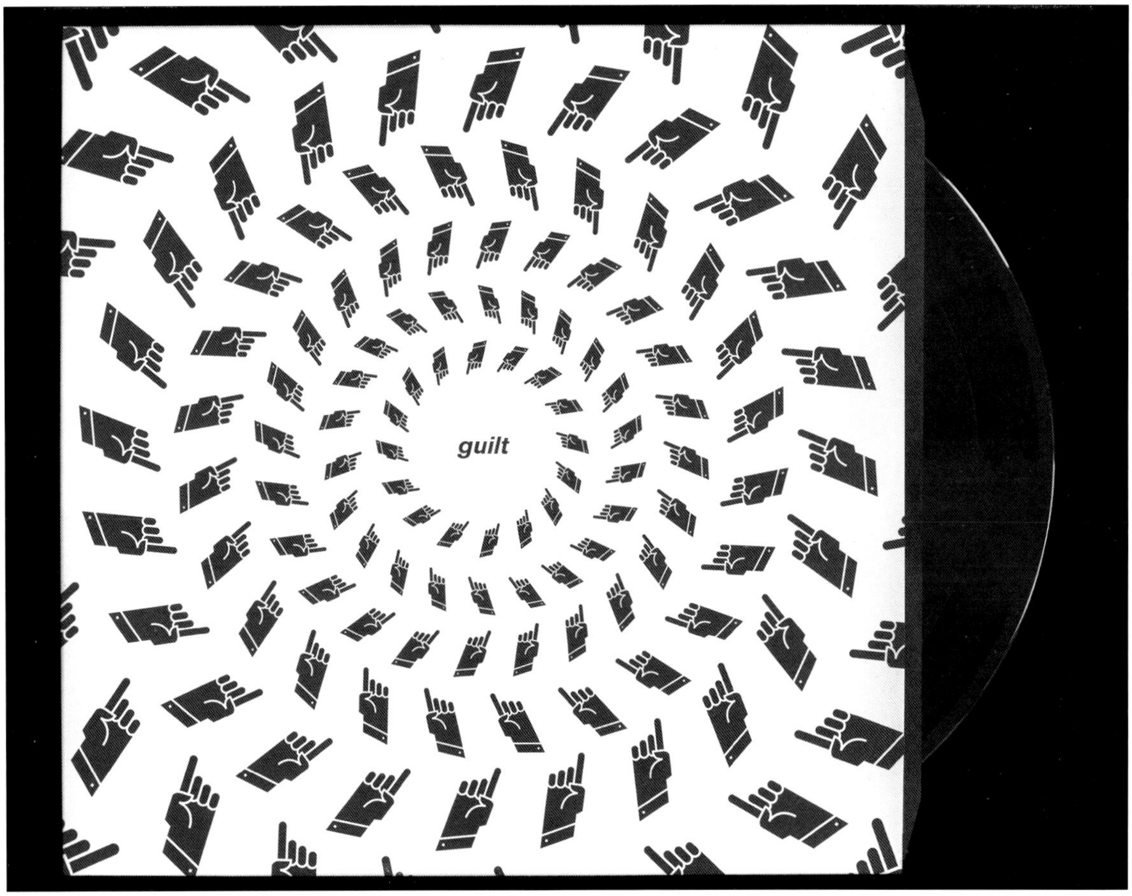
guilt

guilt
darius vaikas
guilt
A1
guilt
B1
no regrets

Designer Lee Robinson has always had a fascination with optical illusions. Affected by Escher and Bridget Riley, he designed these op art works with simple lines.

Visual perceptions can be tricked. In these images, the designer influenced the way the eyes perceive lines, colors, and forms to fool vision, making us feel the space that does not exist in the images.

UNTITLED OP ART

Design: Altered Tv ltd

In these abstract geometries, lines are rotated, twisted, and overlapped, creating a visually concave space. Sometimes, the designer even twists the lines into a cylinder, separating the cylinder from the background to create a three-dimensional space.

Inspired by 2-D Pop art paintings, the design team created these 3-D backgrounds on billboards, in magazines, and in newspapers: bringing psychedelic and constructivist worlds to life.

AIZONE 14-16

Design:Sagmeister&Walsh

These backgrounds are filled with optical illusions, they are perspective, rotated, and distorted, bringing out the complex 3-D visual effects and setting off the beauty of the models.

Frooti Fizz is a redesign of two sister brands: Frooti (mango juice) and Appy Fizz (apple juice). Through graphics and animation, the design team aimed to visualize the funky craziness behind the brand.

A library of optical illusion patterns was developed to trick the eyes: they appear to animate and move even when the images are static. These "rotating" patterns show the brand attributes of Frooti Fizz: she's funky- fresh and full of energy.

FROOTI FIZZ

Design:Sagmeister&Walsh

FROOT

This is a VJ LOOP design for creating visual effects at a party. These patterns are just like the rabbit hole in the novel *Alice in Wonderland*, through which the audience seems to enter another magical world.

Cube, sphere, and prismatic perspective are the three main components in this design. Meanwhile, the designer mixes Op art, Pop art, and a special electronic psychedelic trance music to achieve a blended audio-visual enjoyment that brings a fantastic visual feast to the audience.

HYPNOTIC DIGITAL

Design: Electrobacillus EBVJ

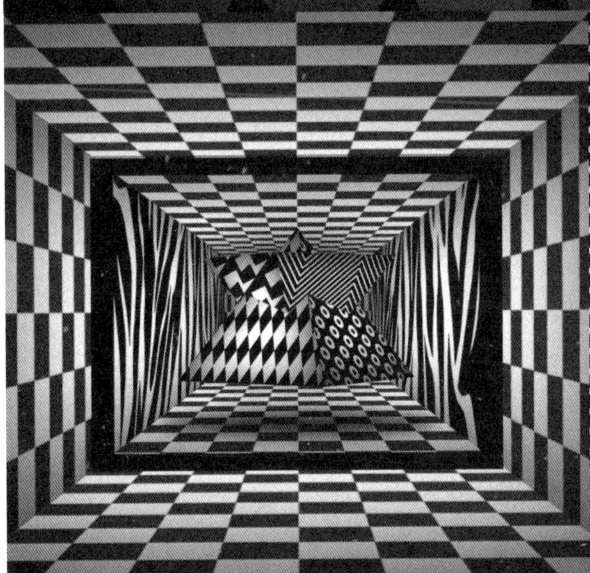

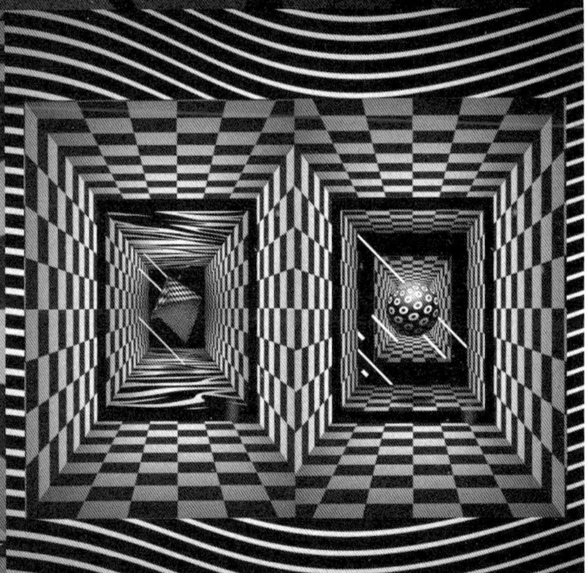

LENTICULAR ILLUSION

The image is arranged into strips, then interlaced with one or more similarly arranged images. Different pictures can be seen from different directions.

Looking from the left, you can see the fish headed to the left.

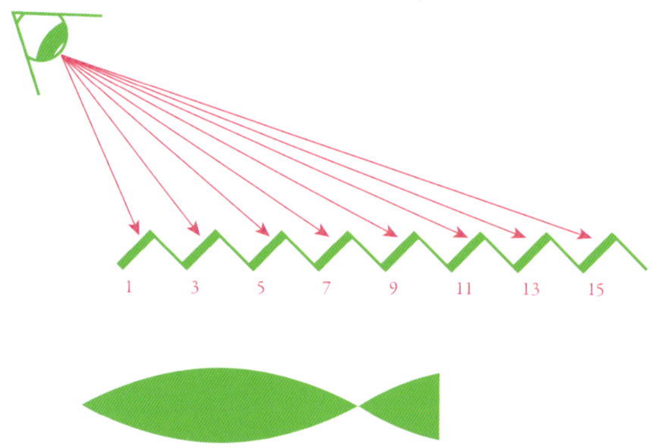

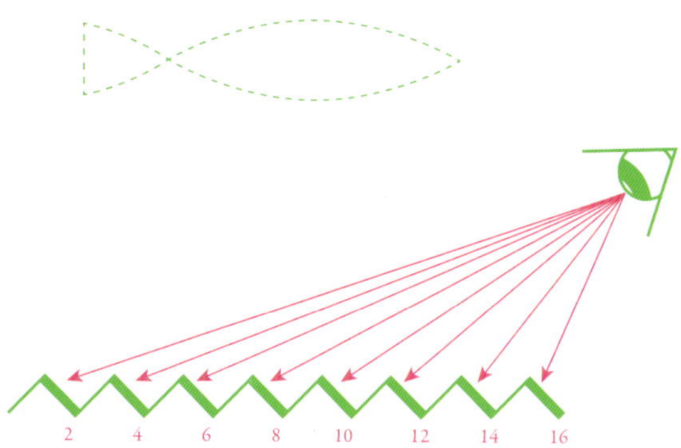

Looking from the right, you can see the fish headed to the right.

DO IT YOURSELF!

Cut along the dotted line on the outer edge.

1 Cut off the graphic on the left.

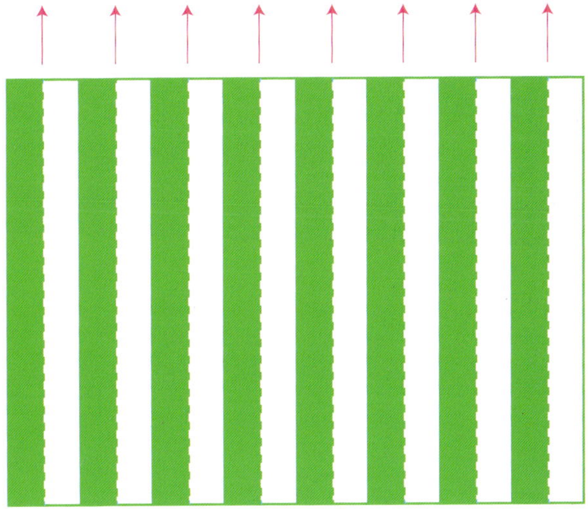

2 Fold the paper forward and backward along the dotted line.

3

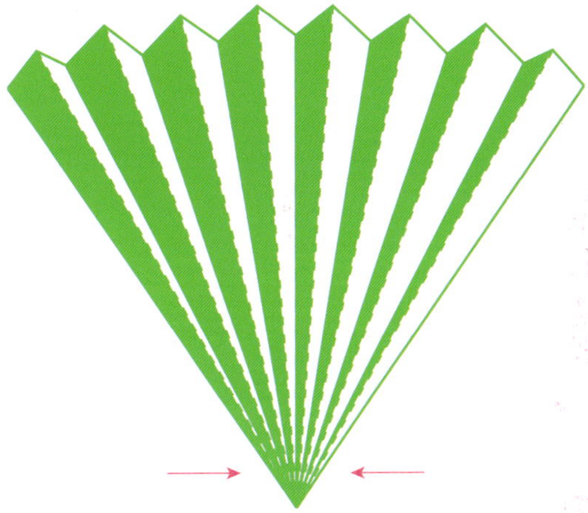

4 Gather the lower end and pinch it with your fingers.

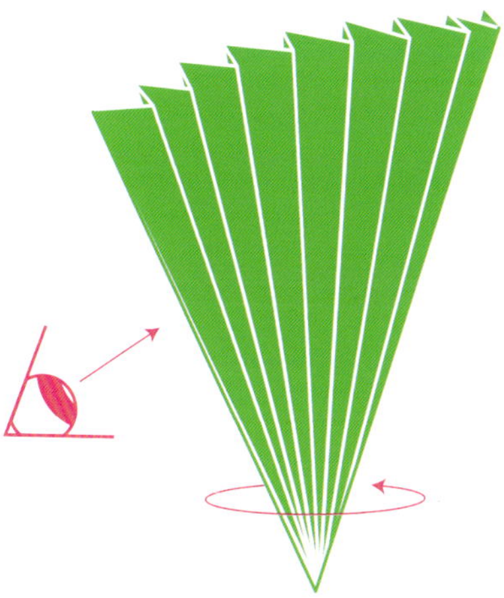

5 Observe it from the left.

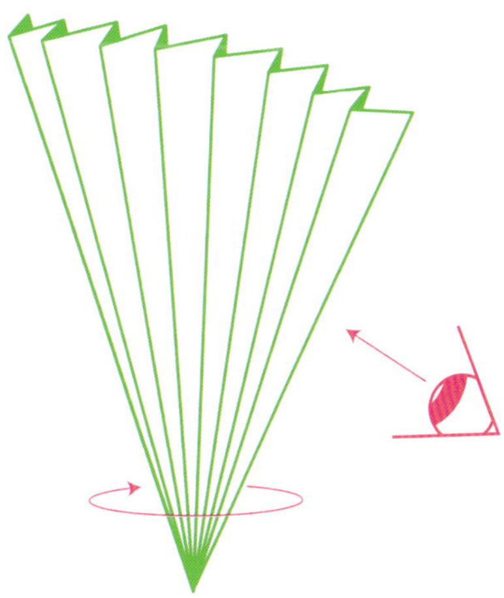

6 Observe it from the right.

NEVER BUILT LOS ANGELES

Design : Clive Wilkinson Architects

To take full promotional advantage of the storefront, the designer used a series of irregular trapezoidal plates to create a large-scale lenticular display, which features two images from different angles.

Pedestrians then encounter the theme of this exhibition—Never Built Los Angeles. When looking from the left, they see only an image of a retrofuturistic flying automobile, a nod to the car culture that has played a significant role in the city's evolution. However, when standing directly in front of the lenticular display, pedestrians encounter the fragmented juxtaposition of the exhibition poster with the retrofuturistic car image.

LENTICULAR ILLUSION & PERSPECTIVE ILLUSION

Overlook Vision

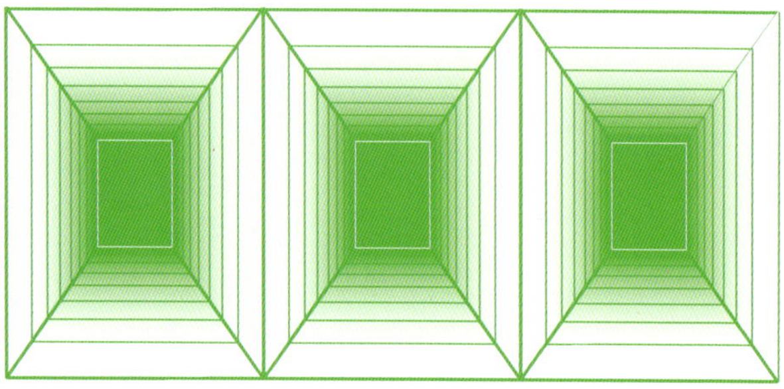

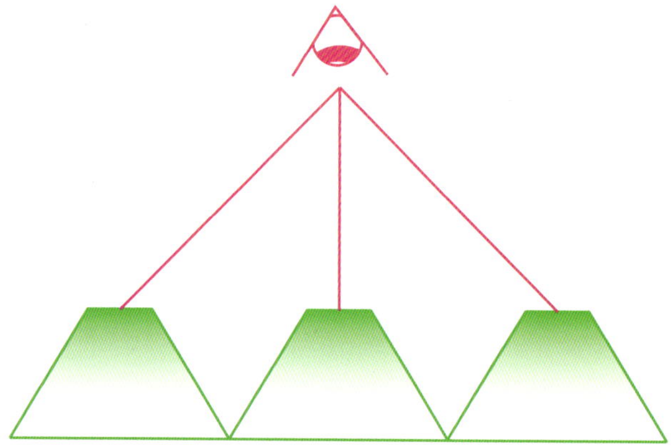

Look down from the center above.

Overlook Vision

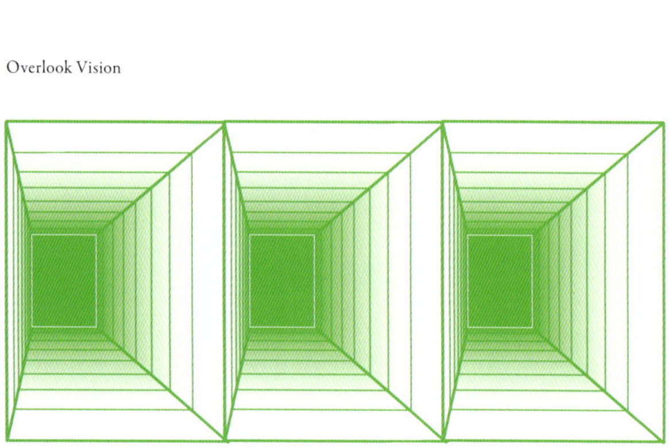

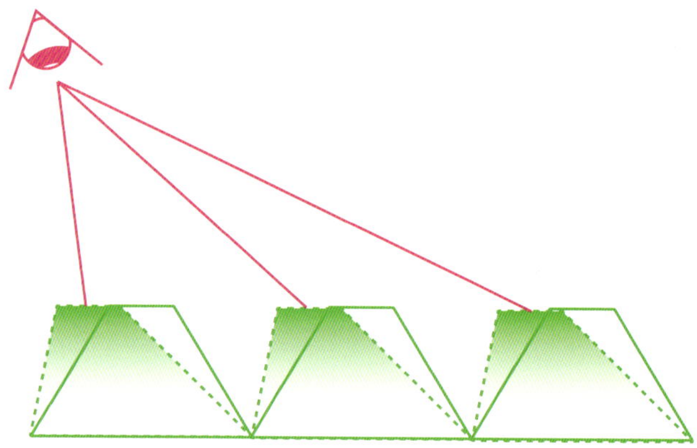

Move from the center to the left.

Overlook Vision

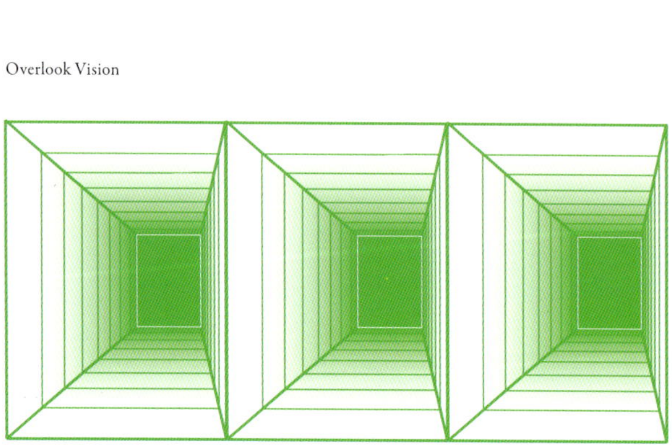

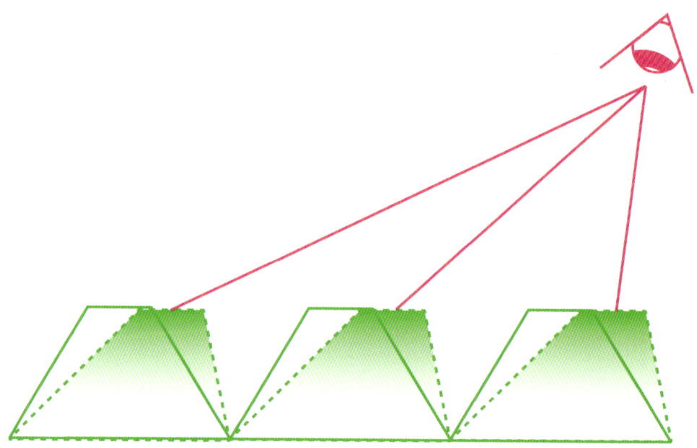

Move from the center to the right.

DO IT YOURSELF!

Cut along the outer edge.

1. Cut off the graphic on the left.
2. Fold the paper backward along the dotted lines.
3. Paste the dotted lines together.

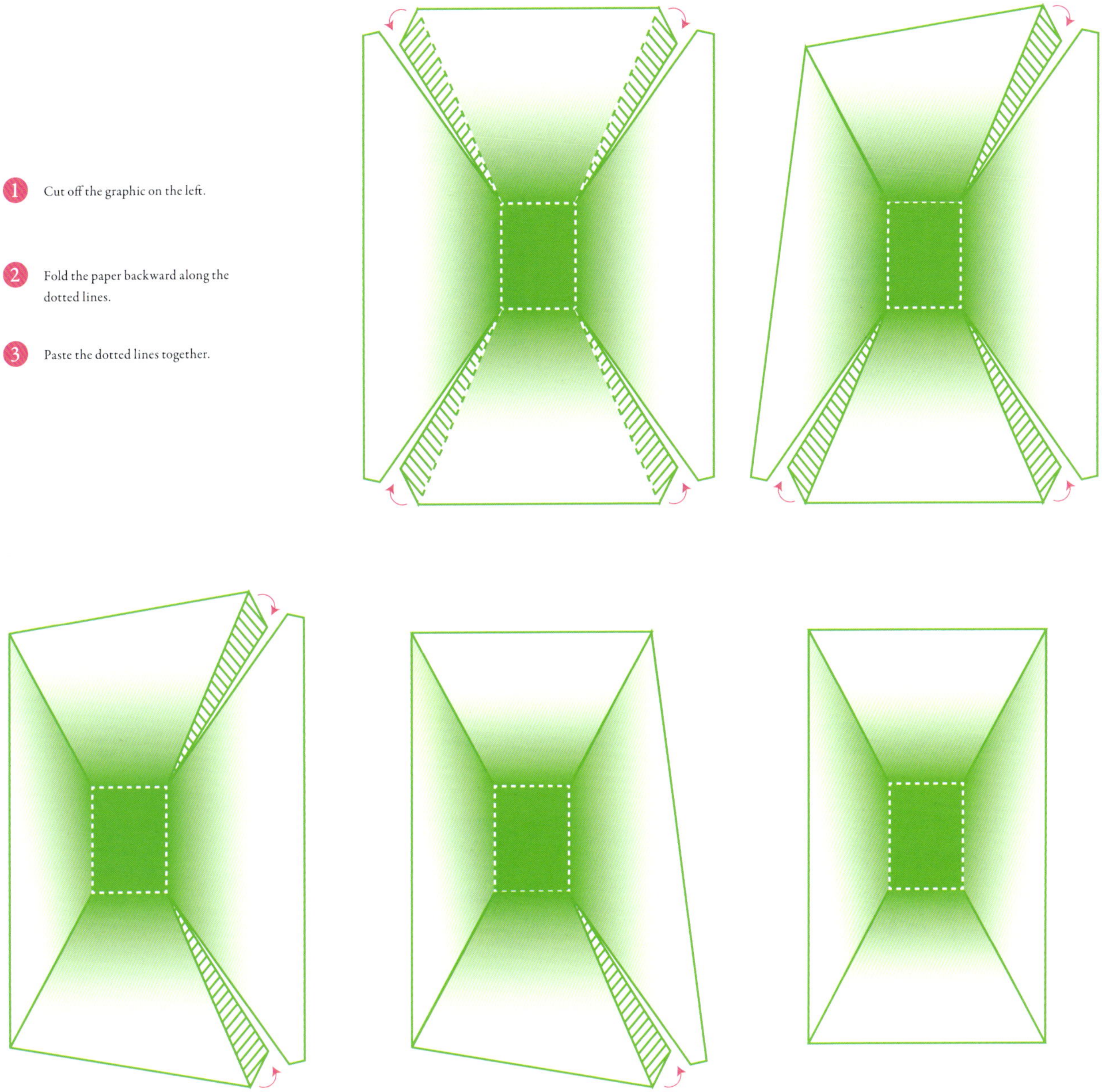

Final Result

- Stereoscopic perspective

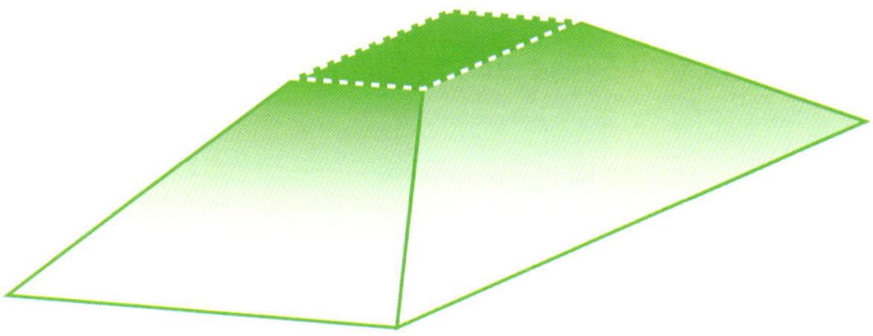

- Front view

- Left view

In Reverspective, the planes seem to recede.

But, when the viewer moves to the side or up and down, parts of the paintings, walls, and other representations seem to move with the movement of the viewer, but in a reverse direction. This physical illusion is strikingly apparent especially in strong lighting conditions.

REVERSPECTIVE

Design:Patrick Hughes

The designer created wooden lumps of space, which makes the viewers see an uneven three-dimensional scene when walking towards these seemingly flat paintings. Preconceived assumptions of eye and brain are challenged. These works greatly change the way we perceive space.

FORD DYNAMIC LED HEADLIGHTS PRESENTS

ADAPTIVE POSTER

TRANSLATION:

Ford Mondeo with Adaptive LED Headlights.

Headlights that steer as you do.

FORD ADAPTIVE POSTER

Agency:Ogilvy Istanbul Executive Creative Director:Selim Ünlüsoy
Copywriter:Erşan Develier Art Director:Burcu Günister

This is a poster designed for Ford, which embodies their goal of creating unique driving experiences.

Consisting of overlapping cutting images, the direction of the tunnel in the poster seems to shift as the viewer moves around it, just as when driving a car.

Go Further

Go Further

Go Further

SIDE VIEW

LENTICULAR ILLUSION & EDGE PERCEPTION

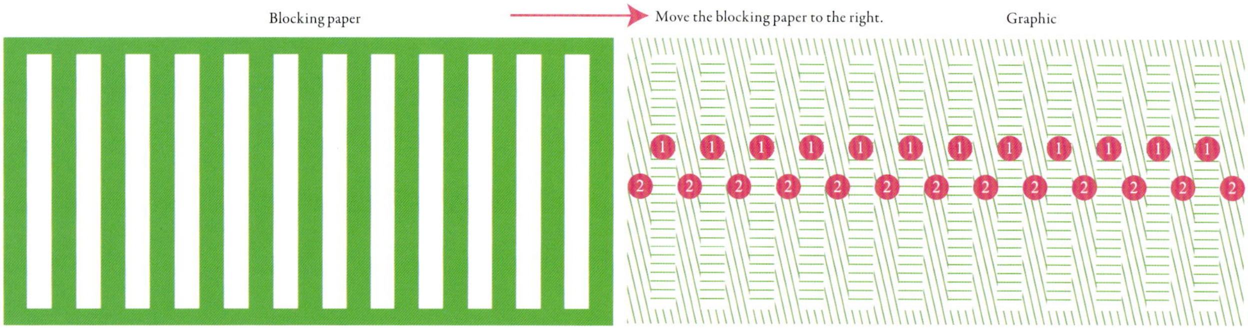

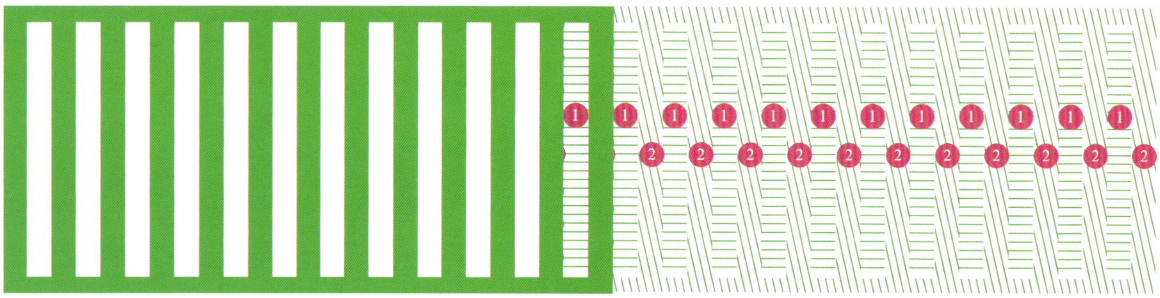

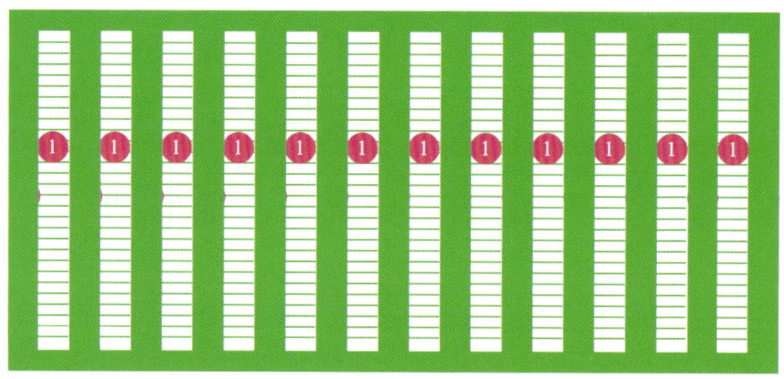

While the blocking paper is moved to the right and covers Graphic 2, Graphic 1 is visible.

While the blocking paper is moved to the right and covers Graphic 1, Graphic 2 is visible.

DO IT YOURSELF!

Cut along the dotted line and cut off the white parts.

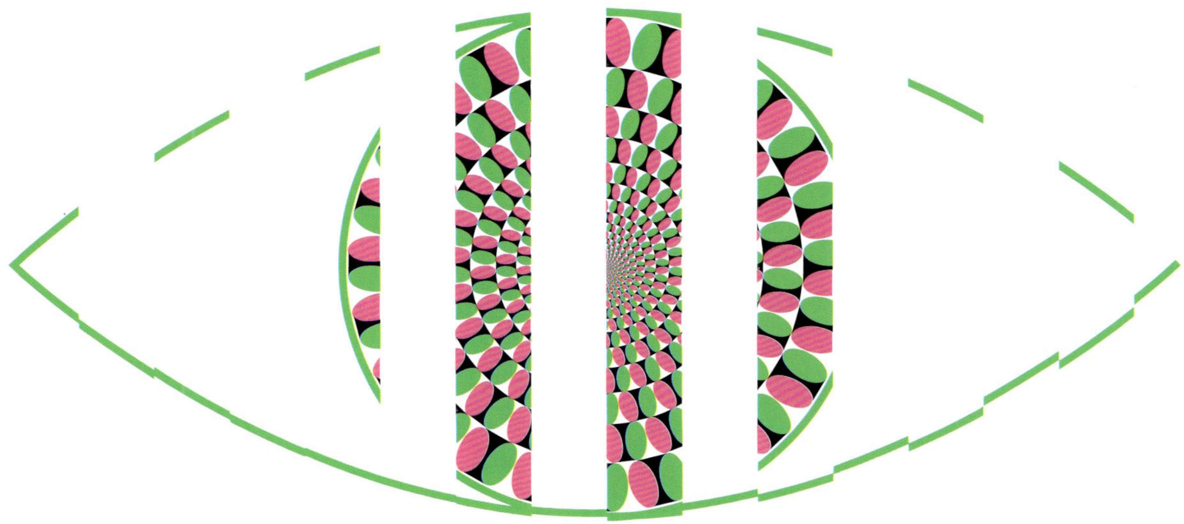

Place the cut blocking paper on the graphic and move it to the right, the graphic is moving !

MAGICIAN'S BUSINESS CARD

Design:Servane Beghin

Inspired by poker cards, Servane Beghin designed this business card for her friend—a magician. Layered and animated optical illusions were applied to the four iconic card patterns (Spades, Hearts, Diamonds, and Clubs). Passing the cards, with a slight offset, through the transparent black and white parallel lines, the four patterns in different colors will magically appear in order.

Besides providing an element of visual surprise, the design can be split into two separate business cards or kept as one.

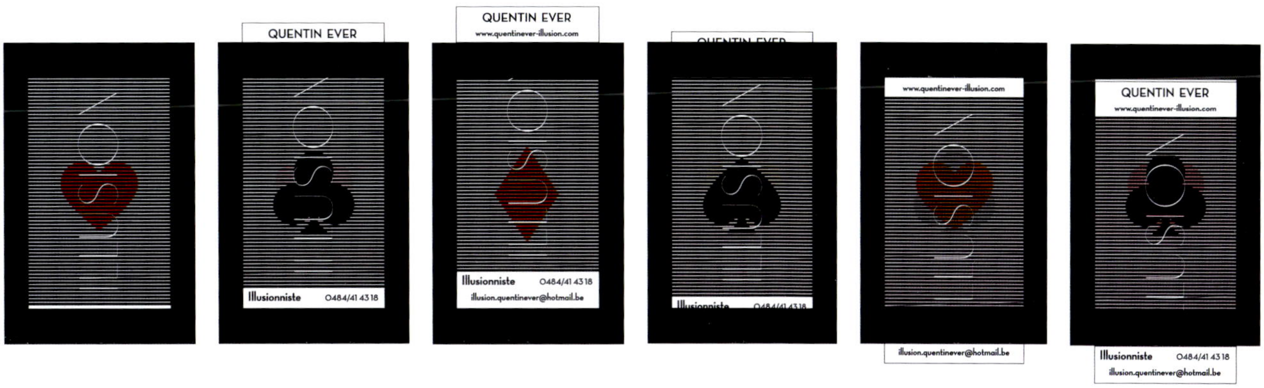

Synthesizing movement with a scan animation technique, this album for Brazilian artist Tulipa Ruiz expresses the dance-friendly nature of music.

As the Portuguese title Dancê suggests, designer Tereza Bettinardi placed the illustrations behind the striped jacket. The rapid alternation of two different drawings creates an illusion of dancing movement by pulling the jacket. This old scan animation technique brings the illustrations to life.

DANCÊ, TULIPA RUIZ

Design:Tereza Bettinardi

RUIZ
DANCE

RUIZ
DANCE

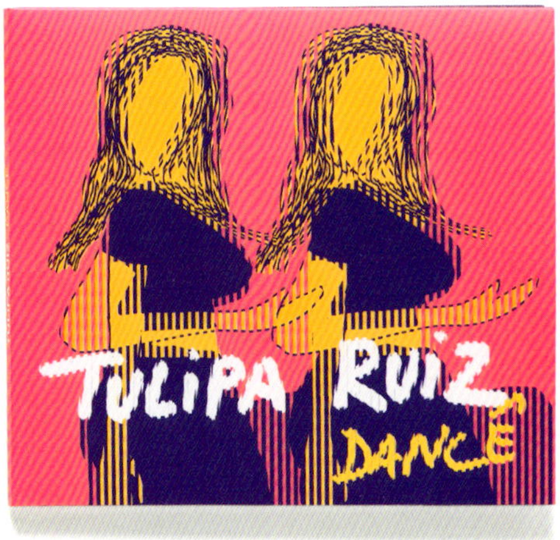
TULIPA RUIZ
DANCÊ

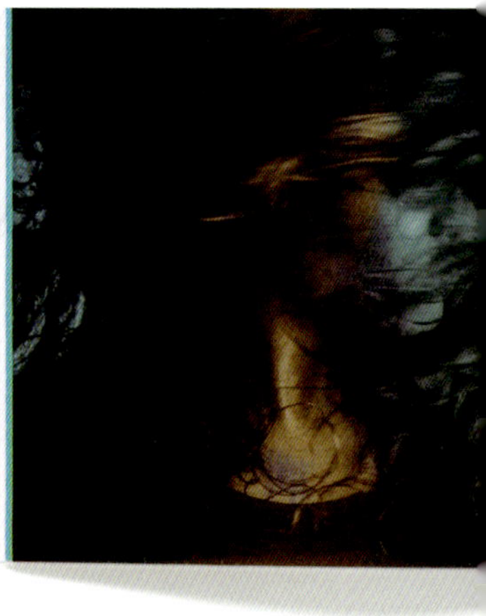

9. FÍSICO
3:42 | BR 5RQ 15 00005
Tudo que eu gosto tá em você. É puramente físico. Tudo tá em você, físico. Tudo que eu gosto tá em você. É puramente físico. Tudo tá em você, físico. Tem a ver com a soma de tudo que há. O formato do nariz. Osso pontudo do pescoço. Lóbulo da orelha. Desenho da sobrancelha. Pintas pela pele. Pelos, tornozelo. Dedo, nuca, calcanhar, cabelo. Da boca pra fora. Fora de fora pra dentro. Um frio na barriga. Fora o aperto no peito. Da boca pra fora. Fora de fora pra dentro. Você veio assim sem defeito.
música: Tulipa Ruiz e Gustavo Ruiz, voz: Tulipa Ruiz, guitarra: Gustavo Ruiz, baixo, guitarras e sintetizadores: Kassin, bateria, afoxé, pandeirola, agogô e drum fills: Stephane San Juan.

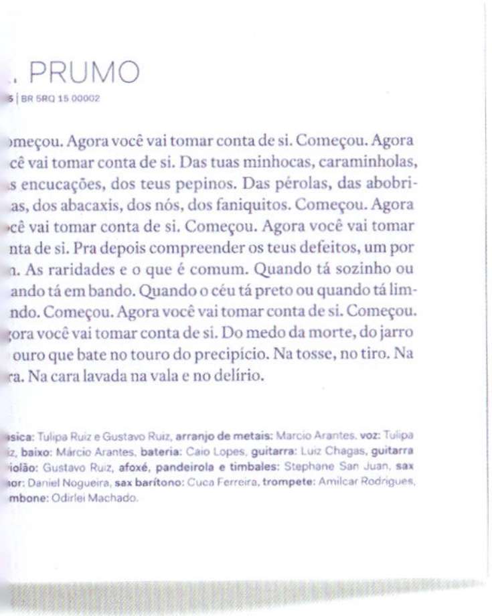
. PRUMO
s | BR 5RQ 15 00002
omeçou. Agora você vai tomar conta de si. Começou. Agora
cê vai tomar conta de si. Das tuas minhocas, caraminholas,
s encucações, dos teus pepinos. Das pérolas, das abobri-
as, dos abacaxis, dos nós, dos faniquitos. Começou. Agora
cê vai tomar conta de si. Começou. Agora você vai tomar
nta de si. Pra depois compreender os teus defeitos, um por
. As raridades e o que é comum. Quando tá sozinho ou
ando tá em bando. Quando o céu tá preto ou quando tá lim-
ndo. Começou. Agora você vai tomar conta de si. Começou.
ora você vai tomar conta de si. Do medo da morte, do jarro
ouro que bate no touro do precipício. Na tosse, no tiro. Na
a. Na cara lavada na vala e no delírio.
sica: Tulipa Ruiz e Gustavo Ruiz, arranjo de metais: Marcio Arantes, voz: Tulipa
z, baixo: Márcio Arantes, bateria: Caio Lopes, guitarra: Luiz Chagas, guitarra
iolão: Gustavo Ruiz, afoxé, pandeirola e timbales: Stephane San Juan, sax
or: Daniel Nogueira, sax barítono: Cuca Ferreira, trompete: Amilcar Rodrigues,
mbone: Odirlei Machado.

4. ELIXIR
4:07 | BR 5RQ 15 00003
Dormir é o meu sonho principal. Fechar os olhos sem ter para onde ir. Dormir é o meu sonho principal. Fechar os olhos sem ter para onde ir. Zero reflexão, zero. Zero reflexão, zero. Zero reflexão, zero. E entra no estado zen. Zero reflexão, zero. Zero reflexão, zero. Zero reflexão, zero. E entra no estado zen. Apaga, filtra, manera. Massageia o esqueleto. A cuca, a cabeça, a traqueia. Cotovelo do esqueleto. A lombriga, clavícula, pé e a costela do esqueleto. Dormir é o meu sonho principal. Legado aos olhos como se fosse elixir. Dormir é o meu sonho principal. Legado aos olhos como se fosse elixir. Zero reflexão, zero. Zero reflexão, zero. Zero reflexão, zero. E entra no estado zen. Zero reflexão, zero. Zero reflexão, zero. Zero reflexão, zero. E entra no estado zen.
música: Tulipa Ruiz e Gustavo Ruiz, arranjo de metais: Jacques Mathias, voz: Tulipa Ruiz, baixo: Marcio Arantes, bateria: Caio Lopes, guitarras: Gustavo Ruiz e Luiz Chagas; guizo, shaker, coquinho, bongô, campana, clave e conga: Stephane San Juan, sax tenor: Daniel Nogueira, sax barítono: Cuca Ferreira, trompete: Amilcar Rodrigues, trombone: Odirlei Machado, trompa: Mário Rocha.

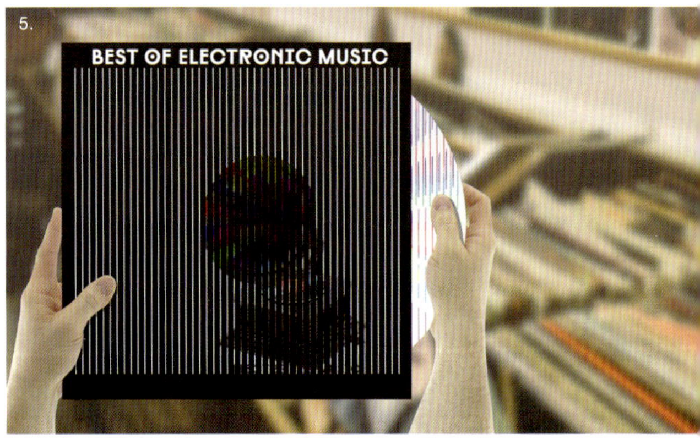

This cover design of a music record collection is filled with shaded and wide black stripes and transparent narrow strips. Ten color images of the gramophone are applied on the musical plate. While the plate is moved out from the cover in the corresponding rhythm, an illusion occurs. It creates an illusion of movement and animation of the gramophone.

MUSIC RECORD COLLECTION OF ELECTRONIC MUSIC

Design:Roma Rehin

NIC MUSIC
ELECTRONIC MUSIC

BEST OF ELECTRONIC MUSIC

7.

BEST OF ELECTRONIC MUSIC

PERSPECTIVE ILLUSION

While observing objects under the effect of perspective discipline, visual illusion occurs because of the observer's differences in height and distance.

1 Draw the outline of the letter "F" and draw a point in the distance as a "far point."

2 With a ruler, connect each corner of the outline of the letter "F" to the "far point."

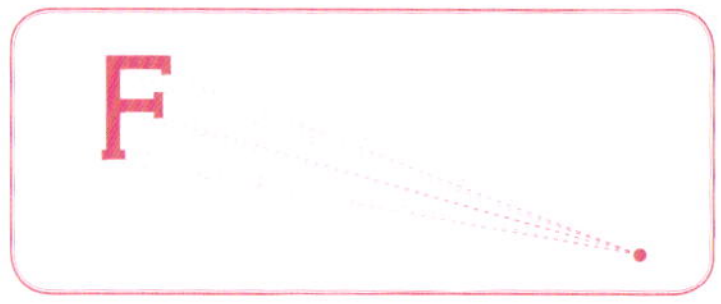

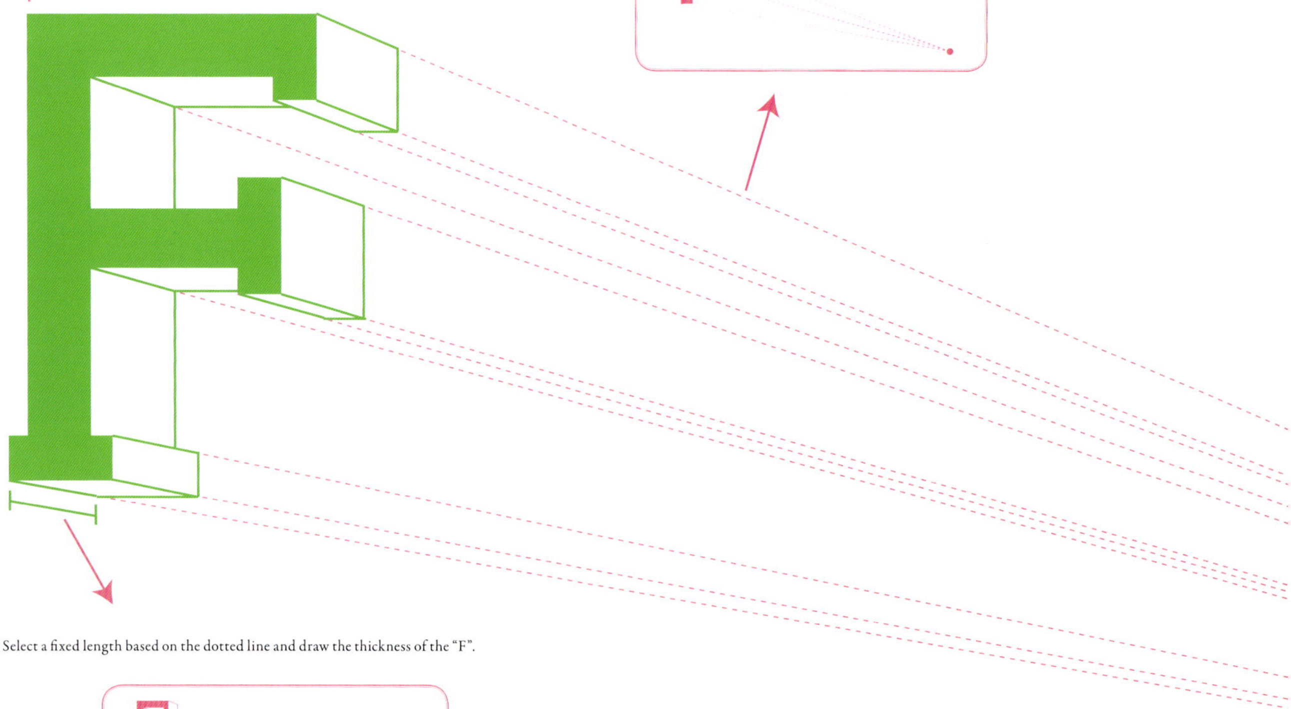

3 Select a fixed length based on the dotted line and draw the thickness of the "F".

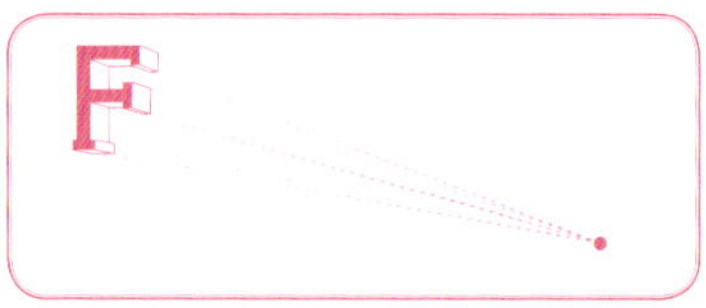

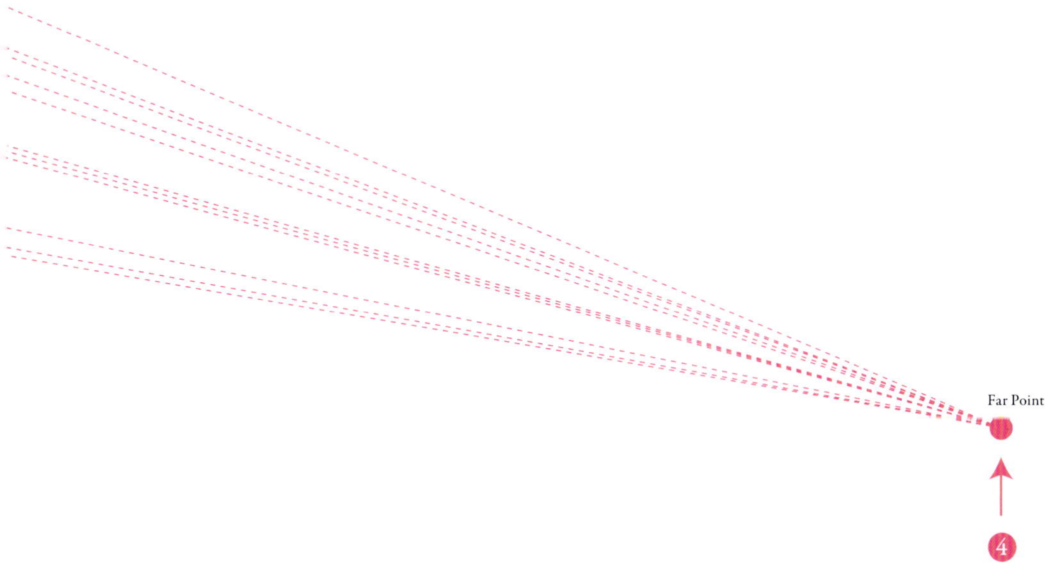

Take a picture of "F" above the "far point" and adjust the angle of the camera slightly to see the three-dimensional "F".

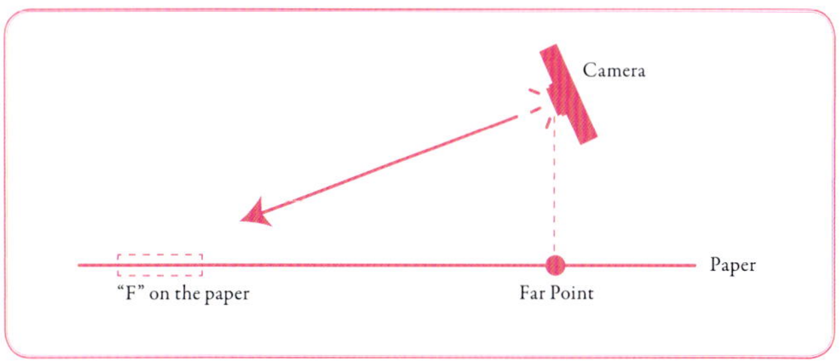

1 Fold a piece of paper and make a crease.

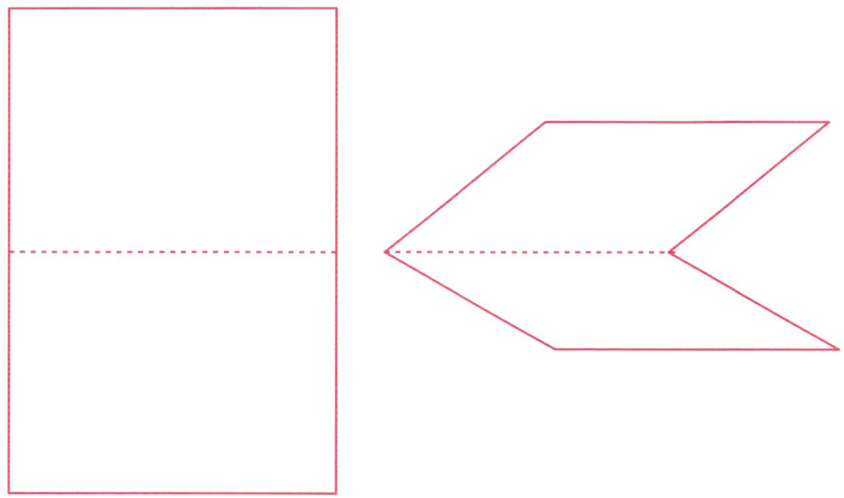

2 Take the crease as the center line and draw a rectangle.

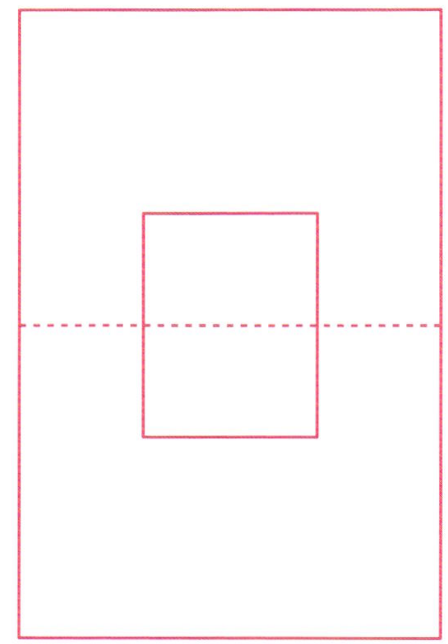

3 Draw a cube as a reference and fold the paper at an angle parallel to the line A-B.
Draw the Point a and Point b on the paper.

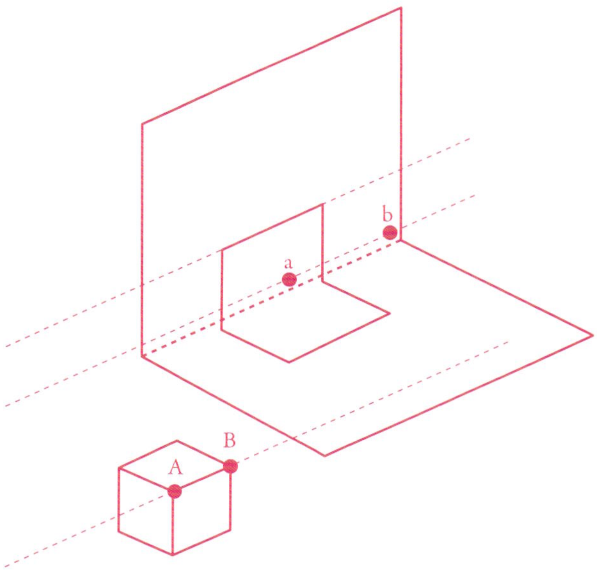

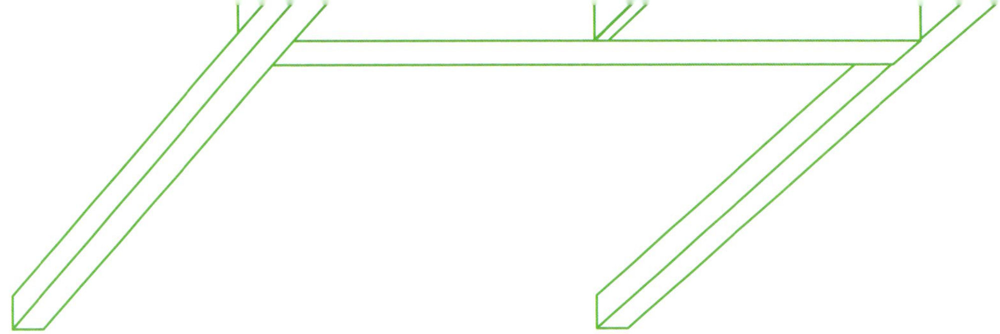

4. Connect the lines as shown below. (Line a-c is perpendicular to line c-d, and line b-d is perpendicular to line c-d.)

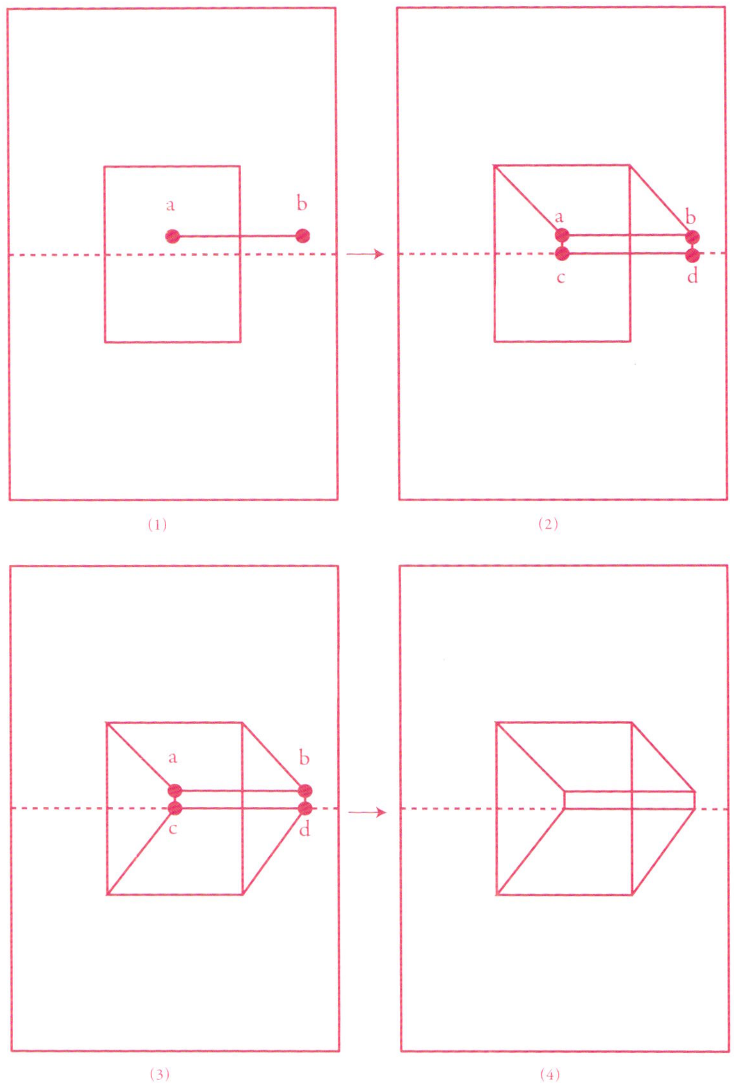

★ Fold the book (at about 90°)and look from the proper angle, you can see a three-dimensional table.

5. Fold the paper and adjust the angle. You can see a cube on the paper.

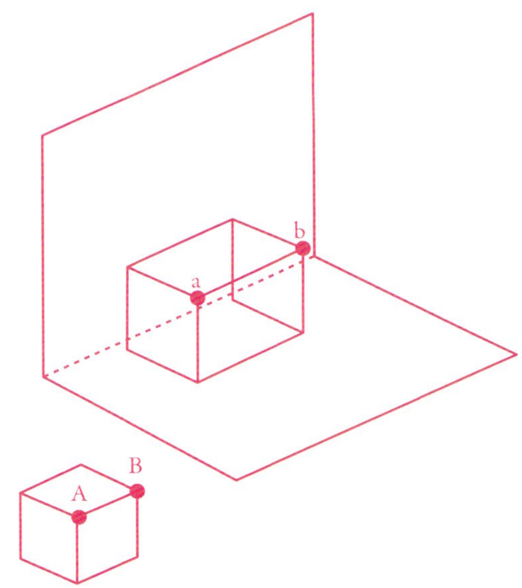

Ramon Bruin likes artistic creations that combine drawing with photography. Drawing on paper, cardboard, wood panel, and canvas, Ramon can make the simplest drawing become vivid, interesting, and complex 3-D artwork.

3-D ILLUSION

Design: Ramon Bruin

RamonBruin

Panels are painted in acrylics to stretch the boundaries of visual illusion. Then different shadows, angles, and perspective methods are used to connect the drawing with reality, making a three-dimensional effect. These visual illusion drawings are colorful and bold, sometimes with a hint of sarcasm.

Ramon Bruin 2015

ROOK Groep
Ramon Bruin 2014

ROLLS ROYCE
Ramon Bruin 2014

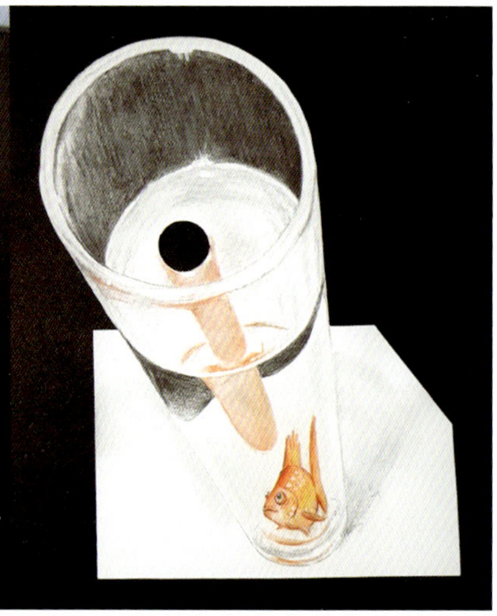

Designer Alessandro Diddi combines practical aspects (design, photography, and lighting) with psychological aspects (what the observer perceives) in his anamorphic drawings, creating an illusion in which two-dimensional drawings appear to be three-dimension when viewed from a single point of view.

With photography and lighting effects, some real items such as a pencil, fingers, and a ring are inserted in the graphite on paper, which makes people see the drawing "come out" from the paper.

ANAMORPHIC PHOTOGRAPHED DRAWINGS

Design: Alessandro Diddi

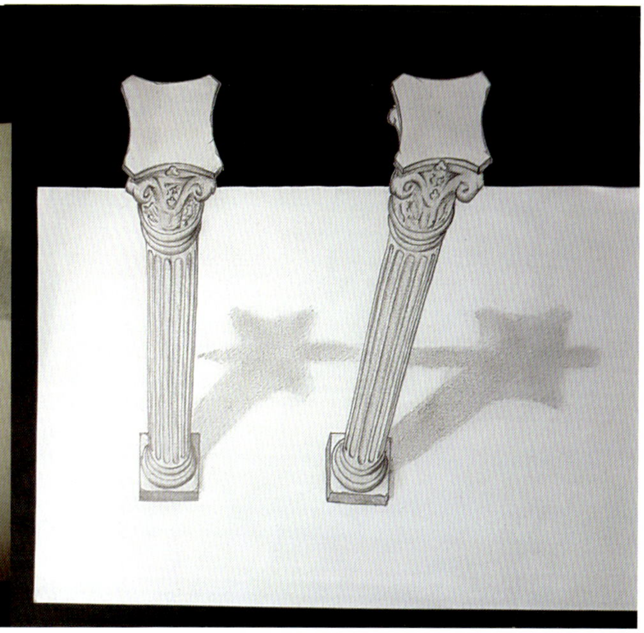

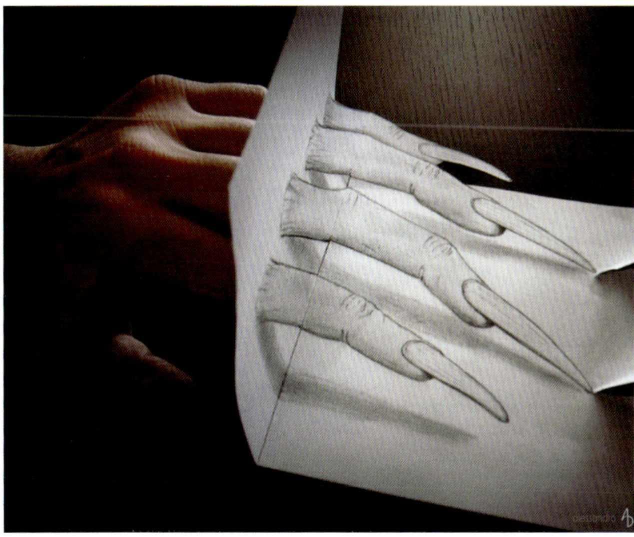

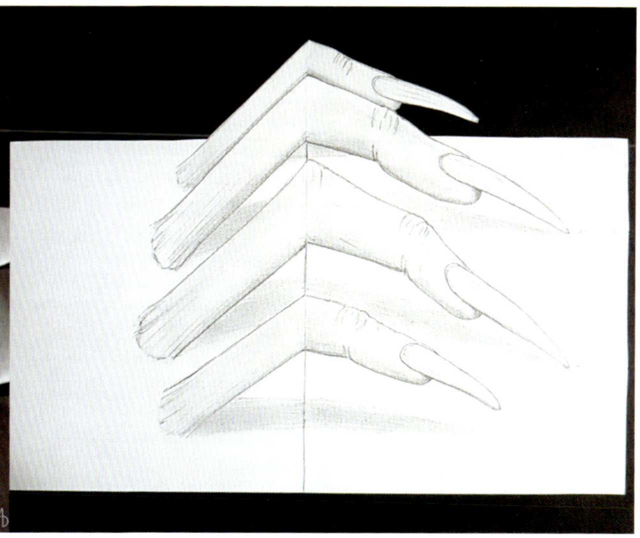

Designer Hideyuki Nagai tends to use the most ordinary painting materials, such as pencil and paper, to create surprising art by using analog methods.

3-D PENCIL ART

Design: Hideyuki Nagai

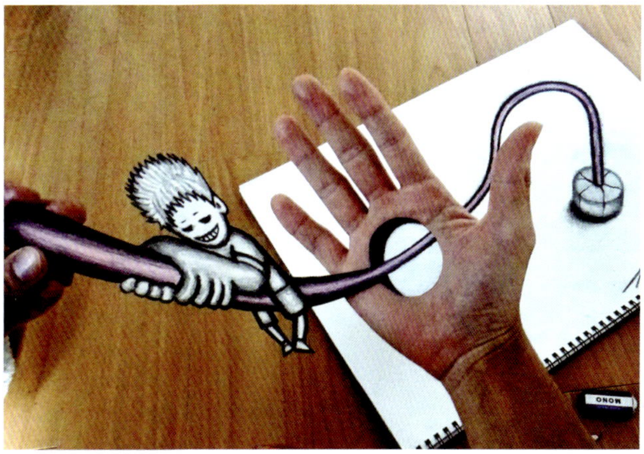

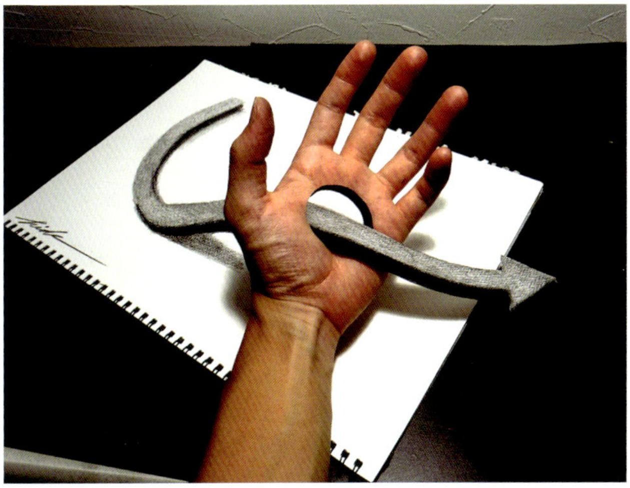

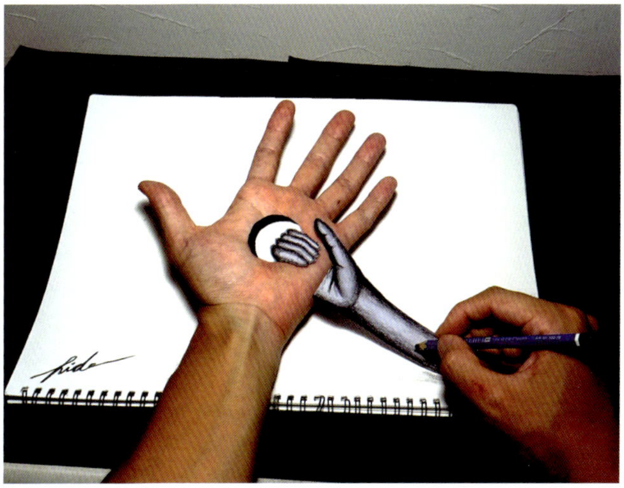

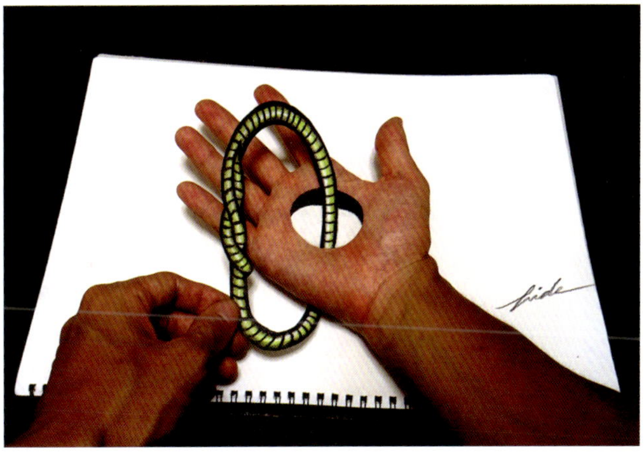

He usually divides his pencil art into two parts: the paper and his hand.

First, he cuts the white paper into a circle and draws the shadow along the edge of it, creating the illusion of a hole. Then he puts the circle on his hand and draws the other parts of the art on the paper, putting the hand and the paper together, which makes the painting seem to be able to pass through the palm, while looking from a certain angle.

These modern calligraphy and lettering artworks are based on a traditional Russian ligature style. The peculiarity of this lettering is the traditional old Cyrillic script. Artist Dmitry Lamonov tried to rethink it in a modern manner, by combining his calligraphy style with illusions. To make the letters outside of the frame of paper, he distorted the letters by using some graphic editors to make the lettering collages from the pictures.

CALLIGRAPHY 3-D ILLUSIONS

Design: Dmitry Lamonov

DUBAI CANVAS 2014
-ABSEILING THE BURJ KHALIFA

Design: Tracy Lee Stum

This work was inspired by death, fearless courage, and skydiving. Designer wanted to create the moment that participants are about to slide down the high city tower.

Created with chalk pastels, this work of art was created using a forced perspective technique. There is a vanishing point located at the center bottom of the wall image. With all vertical lines on the ground converging to this spot, the illusion of extreme depth is created when the viewer looks at it from a low position.

GOUTTES À DOUTES

Design: François Abelanet

Created beside the Angers Castle, this incredible artwork imitates the vibrations, shapes, and waves of a moat.

The old stones seem to awaken, the ramparts to move, and the people can almost hear the murmur of the water. The surprising paradox is revealed once people look at it from different angles.

The theme of this project is biodiversity.

While standing on this huge geometrical figure, the viewer can find that the proportions are confusing, the shadows unusual, and the classic geometry appears warped.

WHERE ARE WE?

Design:François Abelanet

This is an ephemeral garden created for the City of Paris to draw public attention to respect for nature and the trees in the city.

This giant 3-D axial anamorphosis on the City Hall's esplanade was covered with trees and grass, suggesting the beauty but also fragility of this planet. The designer transformed the confusing sight into a perfectly circular globe via a specifically calculated viewpoint.

WHO TO BELIEVE?

Design:François Abelanet

ARCHIVES
DE LA VIE
LITTÉRAIRE
SOUS
L'OCCUPATION

Inspired by the idea that leaves are reborn every year then disappear once again, the designer created this anamorphic installation to show the fragility of nature and demonstrate that people must protect it at all costs for fear of it disappearing forever.

This installation represents more than 2,000 plants spread out in geometrical shapes sprouting out of the ground, reminding people that they must push for more vegetation in cities, pay homage to nature, and aspire for change—a change of attitude towards eco-systems and environment, a change in the way they live their lives.

ARMONIA Y NATURALEZA

Design:François Abelanet

POOL, LOSS OF COLOR

Design:Jeroen Bisscheroux

POOL, LOSS OF COLOR is an artwork commemorating the Great Tohoku Earthquake of 2011, and the tsunami that caused the Fukushima Daiichi nuclear disaster.

This artwork is a tile carpet showing the proportion of a real swimming pool. The outskirts of the carpet are made of white tiles, like the edge of a swimming pool. Inside the carpet, the designer uses black shadow and a linear perspective to create 3-D effect, which makes the carpet look like a deep swimming pool.

Except for the blue "water" in the middle, the other parts of the whole work are gray and dark, just like the colorless disaster areas caused by the salty seawater in Sendai after the tsunami.

SoftBank
Mercedes-Benz Connection

"Homesick Camel Klaus's Arrival in Dubai" is a 3-D artwork about a homesick camel called Klaus who once lived in Germany for 3 years. It was created for the Dubai Canvas Festival 2018, and it was a call for imagination and creativity using the additional element of storytelling..

HOMESICK CAMEL KLAUS'S ARRIVAL IN DUBAI

Design:Fredda Wouters

With brush and airbrush, the designer created a realistic effect on the wall. The doors and the camel's legs were drawn on the ground, matching the painting perfectly to the background by copying the real background in the higher corners so viewers cannot recognize the border of the painting. In this way, the designer tried to make the illusion even more real and attractive to people.

PHOENIX INTERFERING THE CONSTRUCTION WORK

Design:Fredda Wouters, Roberto Carlos Treviño Rodriguez

In this artwork, the designers used brushes, rollers, airbrush, and acrylic colors to create a vanishing-point perspective and anamorphosis on the vinyl floor.

The special 3-D effect is produced mainly by the perspectival construction of the bricks of the "columns", the continuation of the escalator, and the painted worker standing on the ladder.

PLAYING WITH DOLPHINS IN A SHOPPING CENTER

Design:Fredda Wouters, Roberto Carlos Treviño Rodriguez

The designers used two principles of visual illusion in this project: a vanishing-point perspective construction and anamorphosis on the ground. The features of this painting are the reflections in "water" and "windows."

Through this surreal artwork, the designers aimed to reopen the minds of spectators to their own imaginations, in which impossible things become possible.

When we were children, our world was always full of fantasy and questions, and we kept trying to discover and understand the world. Today as adults, we seem to have an explanation for everything. We are living in a society in which everything is prepared. Gradually, we are losing the ability to imagine, to build our own ideas, and to use our own creativity. It is time to think out of the box and challenge the regularity.

3-D STREET PAINTING

Design: Cuboliquido

As a versatile 3-D street painter, Cuboliquido was the first artist to combine experiments with anamorphic 3-D art and animated video with video-mapping.

After he experienced graffiti art, he decided to follow the ancient Italian tradition of Madonnari Art,[1] and finally investigating the technique of 3-D art, anamorphic drawing became his first passion. Cubo is good at using perspective and different viewpoints to create three-dimensional space and using shadow to create the floating visual effect.

Underworld Estense Castel Ferrara

[1] Madonnari Art : A pavement art created with chalks and pastels without oil. Pastel is pure pigment, which lends to the bright colors of the paintings in the streets.

Raft of Human Rights

SARASO
TRADING

Magic Show

Acrobat Circus Sarajevo 2012

Swirl of Happiness

Me and Van Gogh

▲ Boy with Marble

▲ La Morra

▲ Floating Girl

▲ Narcussus and His Friends

Refugee La Valletta Malta

▲ Dubai Pearl

▲ Antwerp Deep Sea Diver Tin Toy and the Rubber Plastic Fish

Tin Toy Rocket Space Station

3D ART by cuboliquido

THE PUPPETEER

Design.Vera Bugatti

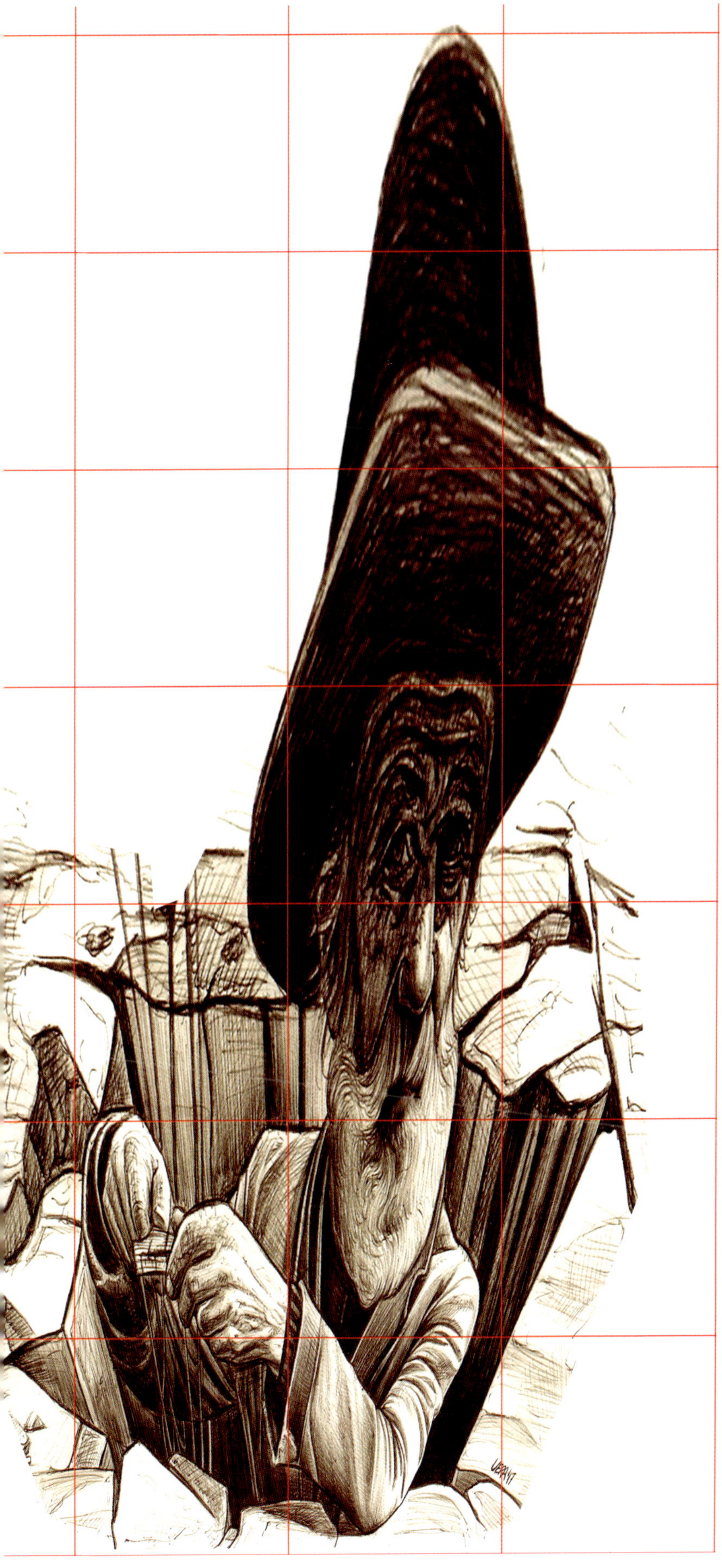

With a bow to traditional Bulgarian puppet theater, the designer invites participants to interact with the painting by posing as a puppet with its hands and feet bound in four real blue ropes. The ends of the ropes disappear in the illusionistic hole and connect with the ropes held in the old man's hand in the painting, which makes viewers see an illusion that the old man in the painting is really driving the participant.

To create the realistic 3-D visual effect, the designer needed to distort the painting.

While drawing, she stood on the viewing point and saw how the painting was growing, to make sure that the proportion of distortion was completely accurate. Then she fixed the rope on the pavement and used it to take on directions of distortion in the painting. The painting is more distorted when viewers go far from the point of view. When viewers get closer to the old man's head, they can find that there is a huge distortion.

DIOSA INDÌGENA DE LA NATURALEZA

Design:Vera Bugatti

This artwork was created in Chiapas, Mexico, which possesses a rich natural heritage.
To demonstrate the biodiversity of the local armadillo and toucan populations the artist chose them as the themes of this artwork.

In the work, an old woman is emerging from a virtual hole with dark water, holding a baby armadillo in her left hand and a green toucan on her head. This old woman with a blind eye is the personification of Nature, who is trying to save the delicate balance between human beings and the environment.

This is a decoration project for the counter of a kitchen. Based on the perspective lines in the background, the text on the counter is "New kitchen," in Cyrillic letters. When viewers walk along the counter from one side, they can catch the 3-D effect.

NEW KITCHEN

Design:Dmitry Lamonov

ВЫХОД
EXIT

1.

3.

ANAMORPHIC ART

Design:Sergio Odeith

Unlike ordinary artists creating scale murals on flat walls, Portuguese artist Sergio Odeith tends to combine graffiti and anamorphic art, creating optical illusion effects by sketching floating objects such as insects and 3-D letters on the 90° corners of walls.

With spray can, he makes these uniquely brilliant pieces seem like popping out the wall and coming alive by using perspective and shading in an obscure style.

1.Greetings from Baton Rouge

2.Private Car Parking -Lisboa

3.Praying Mantis

4.Black Widow

Plastic Tubes

Money Can't Buy Freedom

Anamorphic Chrome Tubes Lettering

Ground Reflection

Dresden 2016

Anamorphic Graffiti Letters

This is an electrical utility box in San Francisco, California, on which Mona Caron painted an anamorphic mural titled *Manifestation Station*.

When people look at this utility box from a specific position, its perspective lines will match those of its surroundings, and the painting on the box is perfectly integrated with the street view. Finally, the box seems transparent and disappears, while also showing the artist's desired changes to the street behind it.

MANIFESTATION STATION

Design:Mona Caron

MONA
CARON
2012

ANAMORPHIC ARTWORK

Design:TRULY | Urban Artists

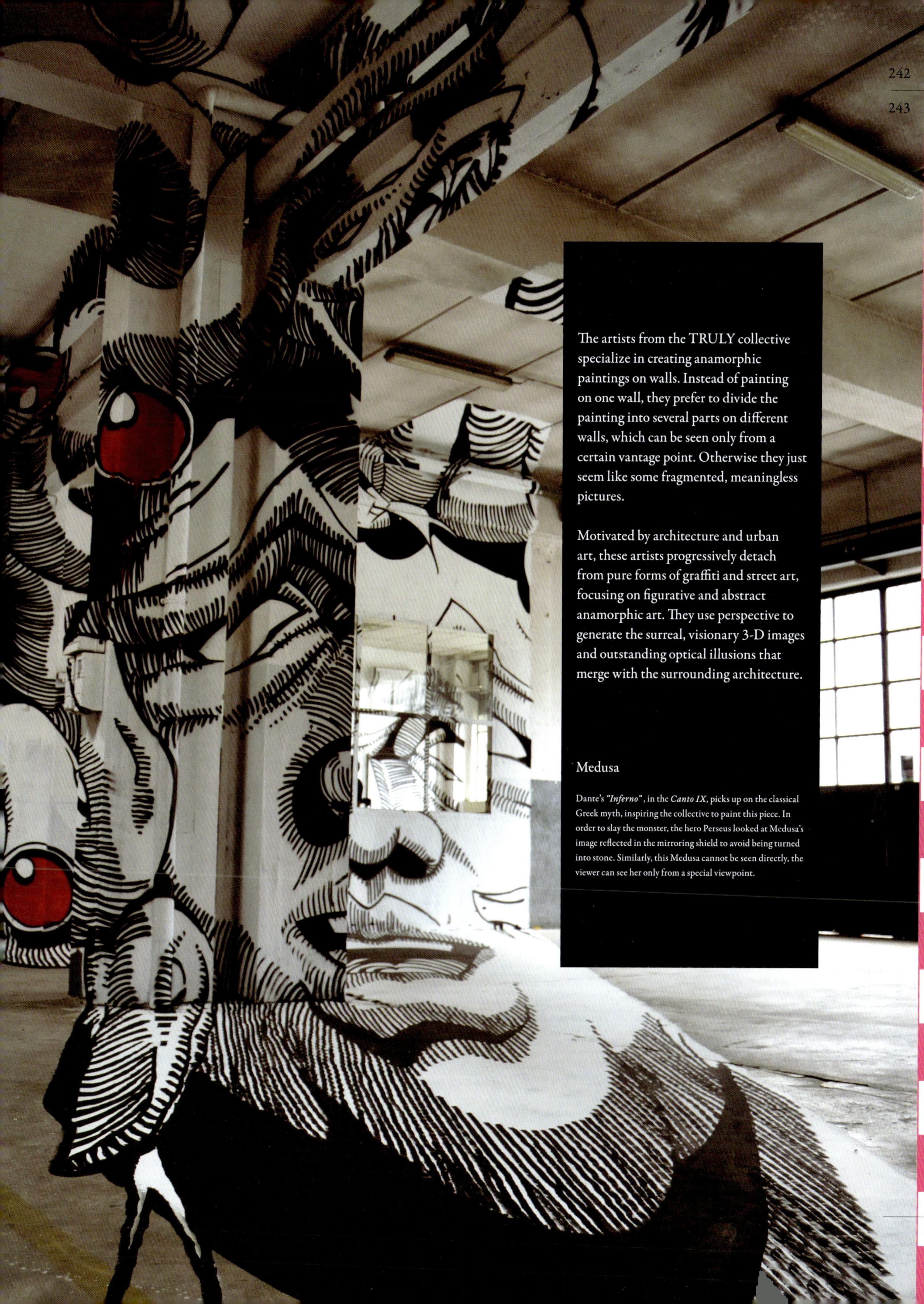

The artists from the TRULY collective specialize in creating anamorphic paintings on walls. Instead of painting on one wall, they prefer to divide the painting into several parts on different walls, which can be seen only from a certain vantage point. Otherwise they just seem like some fragmented, meaningless pictures.

Motivated by architecture and urban art, these artists progressively detach from pure forms of graffiti and street art, focusing on figurative and abstract anamorphic art. They use perspective to generate the surreal, visionary 3-D images and outstanding optical illusions that merge with the surrounding architecture.

Medusa

Dante's *"Inferno"*, in the *Canto IX*, picks up on the classical Greek myth, inspiring the collective to paint this piece. In order to slay the monster, the hero Perseus looked at Medusa's image reflected in the mirroring shield to avoid being turned into stone. Similarly, this Medusa cannot be seen directly, the viewer can see her only from a special viewpoint.

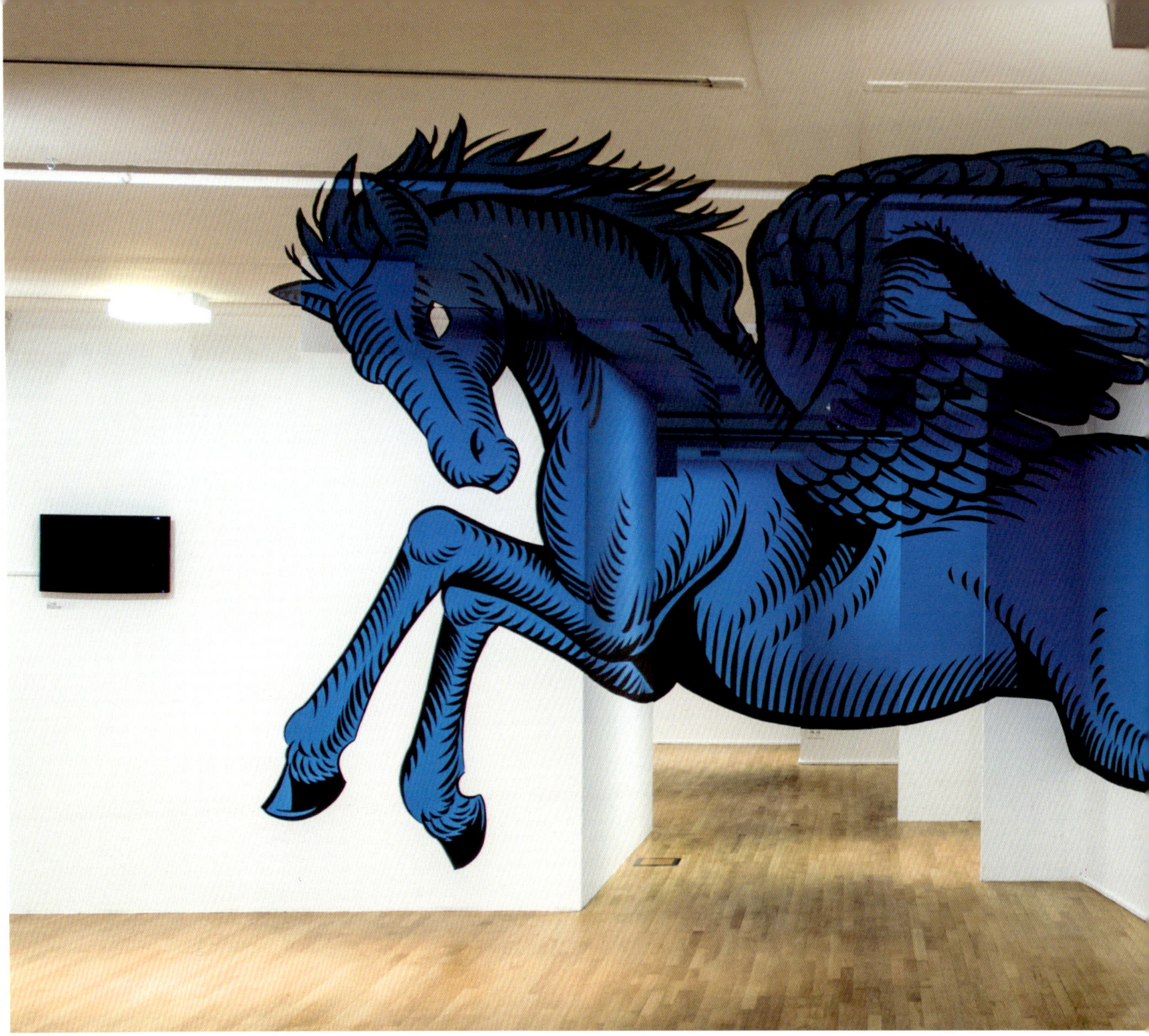

PEGASUS

Design:TRULY | Urban Artists

As a follow-up to the Medusa's popularity, the collective created this artwork, as the myth of the Pegasus is connected with that of the Medusa. The painting was created for the *#Streetart* exhibition, which focused on the conceptual and technical evolution of street art.

This Zeus work "shocks"the space in which it is shown—the EDF Electropolis Museum.

ZEUS

Design:TRULY | Urban Artists

This brightly colored geometric design, part of a mini-series dubbed Supersymmetry, creates a dynamic contrast with the surrounding architecture, a historical palace in central Torino, suggesting continuity between academic tradition and contemporary research.

SUPERSYMMETRY

Design:TRULY | Urban Artists

The colorful circle and cubic border in this design represents global mindset and a multi-faceted world. The collective redefined the boundaries of consciousness in a broader sense.

OUT OF THE BOX

Design:TRULY | Urban Artists

INDEX

ACKNOWLEDGEMENTS

We would like to thank all the designers and contributors who have been involved in the production of this book; their contributions have been indispensable to its creation. We would also like to express our gratitude to all the producers for their invaluable opinions and assistance throughout this project. And to the many others whose names are not credited but have made helpful suggestions, we thank you for your continuous support.

FUTURE PARTNERSHIPS:

If you wish to participate in SendPoints' future projects and publications, please send your website or portfolio to editor01@sendpoints.cn.